# THE GLUTEN-FREE COOKBOOK

# THE GLUTEN-FREE COOKBOOK

## OVER 50 DELICIOUS AND NUTRITIOUS RECIPES TO SUIT EVERY OCCASION

### ANNE SHEASBY

LORENZ BOOKS

First published in 1998 by Lorenz Books

© Anness Publishing Limited 1998

Lorenz Books is an imprint of
Anness Publishing Limited
Hermes House
88-89 Blackfriars Road
London SE1 8HA

This edition distributed in Canada by
Raincoast Books, 8680 Cambie Street, Vancouver, British Columbia V6P 6M9

ISBN 1 85967 585 9

A CIP catalogue for this book is available from the British Library

*Publisher:* Joanna Lorenz
*Senior Cookery Editor:* Linda Fraser
*Designer:* Carole Perks
*Photography:* William Lingwood
*Food for Photography:* Lucy McKelvie
*Styling:* Claire Louise Hunt
*Illustrator:* Madeleine David
*Indexer:* Hilary Bird
*Nutritional Analysis:* Helen Daniels

Printed and bound in Singapore

1 3 5 7 9 10 8 6 4 2

---

NOTES
For all recipes, quantities are given in both metric and imperial measures and,
where appropriate, measures are also given in standard cups and spoons.
Follow one set, but not a mixture, because they are not interchangeable.
Standard spoon and cup measures are level.
1 tsp = 5ml, 1 tbsp = 15ml, 1 cup = 250ml/8fl oz
Australian standard tablespoons are 20ml. Australian readers should
use 3 tsp in place of 1 tbsp for measuring small quantities of gelatine,
cornflour, salt, etc.
Medium eggs are used unless otherwise stated.

NSP is the new term for fibre, it stand for Non-Starch Polysaccarides. Using
older methods of analysis, the recommended fibre intake was 20g per person
per day, using the new method this figure becomes about 11–13g.

---

# CONTENTS

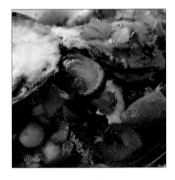

# INTRODUCTION

If you've bought this cookbook, the chances are that you, or someone close to you, has been advised to follow a gluten-free diet. The most likely reason for this is a diagnosis of coeliac disease, but you may have a wheat allergy or a relatively rare skin condition. Whatever the reason, being faced with following a diet for life may seem rather daunting. The good news is that gluten is not particularly difficult to avoid: a huge range of delicious foods remains open to you and you won't need to be singled out from family or friends as everything you eat can be enjoyed by them, too.

## WHAT IS GLUTEN?

Gluten is a protein that occurs naturally in wheat and rye and is related to similar proteins in oats and barley. When the grain is milled, it is the gluten that gives the flour its strength and elasticity. Most people ingest gluten without any difficulty, but in genetically susceptible individuals, it can cause problems.

## COELIAC DISEASE

This life-long condition, caused by a sensitivity to gluten, affects about one in 1,000 to one in 1,500 people world-wide. Coeliac disease was once thought of as a disease exclusive to childhood, but while the condition is present from birth, the symptoms may not appear until much later in life. Nowadays, far more adults than children have the condition; the majority of newly diagnosed coeliacs are aged between 30 and 45, with a significant number falling in the over-60s category.

The condition is known to run in families, and some coeliacs without obvious symptoms are detected when their relatives are being studied. It is suspected that many cases of coeliac disease remain undiagnosed, so the number of cases may in fact be higher.

Coeliac disease was first recognized by the Greeks in the second century AD; the word "coeliac" is derived from the Greek "koiliakos", meaning "suffering in the bowels", an apt description of a condition that affects the gastrointestinal tract.

In a person with a healthy digestive system, food that has been broken down in the stomach and duodenum passes through the small intestine, where thread-like projections called

### SYMPTOMS

The symptoms of coeliac disease vary widely, and can be attributable to other medical conditions, so it is vital to seek a proper diagnosis before starting a gluten-free diet.

An adult with coeliac disease may be chronically tired (often due to anaemia resulting from poor iron and folic acid absorption). Mouth ulcers are common, as is abdominal discomfort, often with a feeling of fullness or bloating. Sufferers can be very ill indeed, with vomiting, diarrhoea and severe weight loss. There may be a long history of stomach upsets, or the sufferer may suddenly have developed the condition.

The symptoms of coeliac disease may become apparent at any age. In a baby, for instance, the first sign of a problem is usually about three months, when the child is being weaned. If a child who previously enjoyed his or her feeds becomes miserable at mealtimes, refuses foods and stops gaining weight, medical advice should be sought.

If undiagnosed and untreated, a baby with the coeliac condition will lose weight, become listless and irritable and develop a swollen pot-belly. The stools will be unusually pale, with an offensive odour, and there may be diarrhoea and vomiting. If the condition persists, the child will eventually become seriously ill.

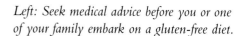

*Left: Seek medical advice before you or one of your family embark on a gluten-free diet.*

villi absorb essential nutrients.

When a coeliac eats food containing gluten, the intestine responds to the food as if it were a foreign body. There is an immune response: the lining of the intestine becomes inflamed and this causes the villi to become flattened. As a result, the surface area is reduced and the gut is no longer able to absorb nutrients efficiently. Over time, weight loss and wasting can occur, leading to malnutrition.

Precisely how or why gluten is harmful to the small intestine is not known, but the only cure for the diagnosed coeliac is to follow a strict gluten-free diet for life. Once gluten is withdrawn from the diet, the flattened villi in the lining of the small intestine will gradually return to normal. Gluten can never be reintroduced, however; once the body has become sensitized to gluten, it will always be affected by it. The occasional minor slip-up may only have minimal effect, but if the diet is not followed strictly and even small quantities of foods containing gluten are eaten regularly, the unpleasant symptoms will return, causing discomfort as well as further damage to the delicate intestine.

If you are uncertain as to whether a given food contains gluten, avoid it. It is simply not worth taking the risk.

When an individual embarks upon a gluten-free diet, the results are sometimes dramatic, but more often he or she will see a gradual but continuing improvement. It takes time for the lining of the small intestine to grow again.

Some coeliacs find that very fatty foods irritate their stomachs; these are often best avoided, particularly in the early stages of the diet. However, it is important not to lose sight of the fact that everyone suffers from illness at some time and a coeliac who feels under the weather may simply have succumbed to a bug that is doing the rounds; before jumping to conclusions, consult a doctor.

## WHEAT ALLERGY OR WHEAT INTOLERANCE AND DERMATITIS HERPETIFORMIS

People suffering from an allergy or intolerance to wheat may also benefit from a strict gluten-free diet, as will anyone suffering from the rare skin complaint known as Dermatitis herpetiformis.

### SYMPTOMS
Wheat allergy or intolerance can cause a wide range of symptoms including aches and pains in the joints and muscles, coughing, sneezing, runny nose, watery and itchy eyes, skin rashes, eczema, faintness and dizziness. The sufferer may have a swollen throat or tongue and find it difficult to swallow. Chest pains, palpitations, nausea, vomiting, diarrhoea, tiredness, lethargy, depression and mood swings have also been reported. Of course, these symptoms can be indicative of all sorts of conditions, and sufferers should always seek sound medical advice before assuming that wheat is the culprit.

If their suspicions are confirmed, however, they should exclude all sources of wheat, including wheat protein and wheat starch. Some sufferers may also react to other grains, such as rye, corn and barley, but unlike coeliacs, many people who are allergic to wheat can tolerate oats.

A product labelled as being gluten-free may also be wheat free, but this is not inevitable; there may certainly be no gluten present, but the product may contain wheat starch. Always check the packaging or seek more information.

Dermatitis herpetiformis – also caused by a sensitivity to gluten – is a rare skin condition that causes an extremely itchy skin rash that consists of red raised patches and small blisters, appearing most often on the elbows, buttocks and knees. The first appearance of the skin rash most often occurs in people who are aged between 15 and 40. The condition is rare in children, although the symptoms can appear at any age.

Dermatitis herpetiformis affects about 1 in 20,000 people (slightly more males than females) and must be diagnosed by a specialist in skin diseases.

Because gluten is implicated, people with dermatitis herpetiformis may also have coeliac disease, although the symptoms will usually be mild. A permanent gluten-free diet will alleviate both the skin condition and the mild coeliac disease, although it may take some time for the rash to disappear entirely.

### DIAGNOSIS
Whether the sufferer is an adult or a child, it is vital that the coeliac condition is properly diagnosed by a doctor before a gluten-free diet is embarked upon.

Diagnosis is by a standard test – a jejunal biopsy – performed under light sedation in the outpatient department of a hospital. A gastroenterologist will remove a small piece of the villi from the lining of the small intestine. Microscopic examination will reveal whether or not the coeliac condition is present.

If the diagnosis is positive, all the patient needs to do to restore the intestine to health is to adhere strictly to a full and varied gluten-free diet. In the short term, the doctor may prescribe a course of vitamins or mineral supplements.

# ACHIEVING A HEALTHY DIET

For all of us, whether we are coeliacs or not, a healthy, balanced diet is basically one that provides the body with all the nutrients it needs for daily maintenance, growth and repair, plus enough energy for daily requirements. A balanced diet should include protein, carbohydrate, fats and fibre in the correct proportions, plus a good balance of vitamins and minerals. Eating well and wisely promotes good health, boosts energy levels, improves resistance and helps to protect the body against heart disease, bowel disorders, certain cancers and obesity.

Most of our dietary problems have arisen because of changes in lifestyle. It is ironic that in an age where food has never been easier to obtain, the desire for instant gratification and "instant" meals has led to an entire industry producing convenience foods that often contain less fibre, minerals and vitamins than home-cooked alternatives, but more fats and sugars. Such foods are tasty, but do not satisfy our hunger for long, so we fill up on snacks like crisps and biscuits.

Variety is the key to a healthy diet. To obtain all the nutrients (including vitamins and minerals) that we need, it is recommended that we choose a variety of foods from the five main food groups every day, and serve them in different ways.

We should be eating plenty of fruit and vegetables (at least five portions daily, not including potatoes). Also on the menu should be cereals and pasta (gluten-free if required), rice and potatoes; moderate amounts of lean meat, fish, poultry and dairy products and only small amounts of foods containing fat or sugar.

We all need to eat less fat (especially saturated fat). Ways to do this include cutting off visible fat on meat, grilling rather than frying foods where possible and looking out for low-fat and reduced-fat alternatives.

Cutting down on sugar and salt is recommended. It is also important to eat regularly (three meals a day), drink less alcohol and take more exercise.

## THE FIVE MAIN FOOD GROUPS

*Above: Meat, poultry, fish and vegetarian protein foods – eat in moderation.*

*Above: Milk and other dairy foods – watch your fat intake.*

*Above: Foods that contain fat and foods that contain sugar – limit these.*

*Left: Fruit and vegetables – aim to eat at least five portions of fruit and vegetables (not counting potatoes) every day.*

*Right: Potatoes, rice, bread, cereals and pasta (gluten-free where needed).*

## DIETARY FIBRE

Some coeliacs worry that, because they are unable to eat wheat and wheat bran, they will not be getting enough fibre. Fibre intake for a coeliac can be increased by adding soya bran or rice bran to food, eating plenty of plain nuts and fresh fruits and vegetables (with the skins left on) and eating brown rice, beans and pulses. Commercially produced high-fibre, gluten-free foods are available.

Before diagnosis, many coeliacs suffer from weight loss and wasting, due to their body's inability to absorb the nutrients from food. However, quite the opposite often occurs once

*Below: High-fibre foods include, clockwise from left, split peas, green and red lentils, wholegrain rice, pinto beans, red kidney beans and mixed nuts.*

a coeliac has become established on a gluten-free diet. The person's appetite returns and food becomes more interesting, so there is a temptation to eat more food than the body needs, resulting in weight gain. Excess weight gain can be a problem for both coeliacs and non-coeliacs alike, and the remedy is the same for both – to follow a sensible diet so that the weight is lost slowly and safely.

When embarking on a gluten-free diet, some coeliacs find it is easier to start simply, with plain foods, such as poached salmon with new potatoes and mangetouts or grilled lamb chops with roasted peppers, followed by fresh fruit desserts. There'll be time enough for more elaborate dishes later, when the cook has mastered the art of making sauces, pastries and puddings using gluten-free ingredients.

## QUICK AND EASY HIGH-FIBRE, GLUTEN-FREE FOODS

All these easy-to-prepare dishes are high in fibre and gluten-free:
- Home-made vegetable, bean or lentil soup.
- A baked jacket potato filled with gluten-free baked beans.
- Corn on the cob.
- A simple salad made from cooked brown rice or buckwheat mixed with diced celery, carrot, tomatoes, yellow pepper, spring onions and walnuts.
- Sticks of fresh pineapple rolled in honey and coated in sesame seeds.
- Fruit salad made from bananas, apples, plums and orange segments, with a few chopped dates and raisins.
- Banana freezies – ripe, peeled bananas spread with honey, rolled in crushed roasted hazelnuts, then frozen on non-stick baking paper.

# FOODS TO EAT AND FOODS TO AVOID

A gluten-free diet excludes all foods containing any form of wheat, barley, rye and oats. (Some coeliacs can tolerate oats with no adverse effects, but many cannot, so it is a wise precaution to exclude it.) Items like bread, cakes, biscuits, pasta and pastries made from wheat flour are obvious sources of gluten, but it is also essential to be aware of less obvious sources, as when wheat flour has been used to coat or dust foods or thicken soups, stews, gravies and puddings. Breadcrumbs, for instance, are used in stuffings and coatings or as a filler in foods like sausages and hamburgers.

## FOODS THAT ARE NATURALLY GLUTEN-FREE

● Fresh or frozen plain meat, fish or poultry, without stuffing or a crumb coating; canned or prepacked plain cooked meats, such as corned beef or ham (without any coating); smoked and cured pure meats; fresh, frozen or cured plain fish or shellfish; fish canned in oil, brine or water.

*Above: Anchovies canned in oil, smoked mackerel and cooked prawns, are all naturally gluten-free.*

● Fresh or frozen plain vegetables or fruit, dried fruit and vegetables (including pulses), plain canned fruit in syrup or juice, vegetables canned in brine, water or juice, plain vegetables pickled in vinegar, potato crisps.
● Eggs (but not Scotch eggs).
● Nuts and seeds of all types, provided they are plain; also peanut butter.
● Gelatine and agar agar.
● Dairy produce including all plain cheeses (but not spreads or processed cheese), milk, dairy cream, natural yogurt, fromage frais; also plain dried milk, evaporated and condensed milk.
● Fats and oils, including pure vegetable oils, such as olive, sunflower and rapeseed; butter, margarine (as long as it does not contain wheatgerm oil), reduced-fat and low-fat spreads.
● Sugar in all its forms, including pure honey, syrup, molasses and treacle.
● Fruit conserves, jam and marmalade.
● Flavourings, seasonings, herbs and spices, including salt, freshly ground black pepper, black peppercorns, cider vinegar and wine vinegar, pure whole or ground spices, tomato purée and garlic purée, pure food flavourings, such as vanilla and almond essences, pure food colourings.
● Breakfast cereals, such as rice crispies, puffed rice, some cornflakes.

*Above: Breakfast need not be a problem for coeliacs. Eggs, jam or marmalade, milk and rice- and corn-based cereals, such as rice crispies and some cornflakes, are all gluten-free. Serve them with gluten-free toast.*

*Above: Add flavour and colour to your meals using black peppercorns, tomato purée, red wine vinegar, pure ground cinnamon, pure food flavourings and colourings.*

● Grains, whether whole or ground, including buckwheat flakes and flour, carob flour, cornflour, gram flour (from ground chick-peas), maize flour, millet flour, potato flour, sorghum flour, soya flour, sweet chestnut flour, teff flour, yam flour, yellow split pea flour, arrowroot, rice (all types including wild rice; also ground rice and rice flour), hominy grits, millet (also millet flakes and seeds), polenta, quinoa grains, sago and tapioca.
● Good quality plain chocolate.
● Yeast (and yeast extract).
● Pure rice noodles, pure corn, rice and millet pasta, pure buckwheat pasta – check that pastas do not contain added wheat flour, starch or binders.
● Drinks, such as tea, coffee, fruit squashes (except barley water), pure fruit juices (preferably unsweetened); also cider, wine, sherry, brandy, port.

## MANUFACTURED FOODS THAT ARE GLUTEN-FREE

A wide range of specially manufactured gluten-free foods is also available. The list includes breads, cakes, biscuits, crackers and crispbreads, plus flours, flour mixes, bread and cake mixes, muesli, pastas and rusks. Talk to your doctor, as in certain countries, such as the UK, you may be able to obtain some of these products on prescription. Others can be purchased from chemists or health food shops, or by mail order, although they can be costly.

Manufactured foods that have been specifically made for the market by reputable companies are very useful. They look like the wheat-flour products they are intended to replace, so will go unremarked at occasions like children's parties.

Many everyday canned and packaged foods are also gluten-free.

When using products, such as gluten-free flours or bread or cake mixes for the first time, always follow the manufacturer's guidance and instructions on usage.

## FOODS TO AVOID

The following foods always contain flour made from wheat, barley, rye or oats, so must be avoided:
● Wheat berries or grains; wheat bran; wheat flakes; wheat flour, such as plain or strong white flour, brown, granary and wholemeal flours; wheat-meal; wheat protein; wheat starch; bulgur wheat; couscous; cracked wheat, durum wheat (used in pasta); kibbled wheat; pourgouri; rusk; semolina; wheatgerm.
● Pearl barley, pot barley, barley flakes, barley flour, barley meal.
● Rye flakes, rye flour, rye meal.
● Oats, oat flakes, jumbo oats, porridge oats, rolled oats, oatmeal, pinhead oatmeal, oatbran, oatgerm.
● Spelt (flour and American pasta made from a grain related to wheat), kamut (Italian wholegrain pasta).
● Triticale (wheat/rye hybrid grain).

## COMMON FOODS THAT MAY CONTAIN GLUTEN

● Dry goods like baking powder, malt, curry powder, mustard powder, MSG (monosodium glutamate flavour enhancer), gravy mixes, spices and spice mixes, pepper compounds and ready-ground white pepper, shredded suet (in packets), stock cubes.
● Pasta (durum wheat pastas are out and some oriental pastas, though made from other grains, contain wheat).
● Some cornflakes.
● Salad dressings, soy sauce, malt vinegar.
● Some processed cheese spreads, some flavoured yogurts.
● Sausages (and sausage rolls), meat pies, beefburgers, pâtés, foods coated in batter or breadcrumbs.
● Dry roasted nuts.
● Communion wafers (gluten-free wafers are available on mail-order).
● Beers, malted milk drinks.

---

*Above right: Some common foods, such as malt vinegar, pasta made with wheat, dry roasted nuts, mustards and malted milk drinks, contain gluten and must be avoided.*

*Below: The range of specially manufactured gluten-free foods includes biscuits, cereal, corn pasta and gluten-free flours.*

### FOOD LABELLING

By law, all manufacturers have to mark or label food with a list of ingredients. Sources of gluten are not always obvious, however. If you read any of the following words on a food label, alarm bells should ring and you should ask for more information: binder, binding, cereal, cereal protein, corn, cornstarch, edible starch, flour, food starch, modified starch, rusk, special edible starch, starch, thickener, thickening or vegetable protein.

# GLUTEN-FREE COOKING

There is nothing special about gluten-free cooking other than the fact that some ingredients are replaced with alternatives that are equally varied and interesting. Once you familiarize yourself with the list of foods that can safely be served (and note the no-no's), it is simply a matter of making delicious dishes that everyone can enjoy. You will rapidly get into the habit of using a variety of alternative starches for baking, cooking, thickening, binding and coating, and in doing so will discover just how delicious many of the less familiar grains can be.

If you are new to gluten-free cooking, you will probably prefer to start with simple no-risk dishes like grills with fresh vegetables. This will have obvious health advantages, but don't turf out the treats. If you continue to serve pies and puddings, cakes and bakes, but make them gluten-free, everyone in the family will be able to enjoy their favourite foods – and the coeliac won't feel isolated.

### USING GLUTEN-FREE FLOURS

Because gluten is the protein that strengthens and binds dough in baking, you may need to find alternative binding agents when using gluten-free flours. Follow recipes for baked goods closely, as they will have been specially formulated to allow for this potential problem. A combination of starches often works better than a single type, and adding egg, pectin powder, grated apple or mashed banana may help to bind gluten-free dough.

### BINDING BURGERS AND SAUSAGES

Although burgers and sausages are conventionally bound with breadcrumbs or rusk, they work equally well without. The best hamburgers are made purely from minced steak, and fresh sausage meat will hold together without additional ingredients. If you must use a binder, add rice flour and egg.

### AVOIDING WHEAT CONTAMINATION

If you are baking a batch of breads, cakes and pastries (only some of which are gluten-free), be careful to keep ingredients separate so that there is no risk of wheat flour contaminating the gluten-free foods. Wash all utensils thoroughly after each use. For a highly allergic person, it may be sensible to use separate baking tins and cooking utensils. Alternatively – and this is simpler and safer – use gluten-free ingredients for all your cooking.

## QUICK TIPS ON GLUTEN-FREE COOKING

● Do not use breadcrumbs (unless they are gluten-free) for coating foods. Crushed gluten-free cornflakes make a good alternative for coating foods and for gratins.

● Do not dust or coat foods with wheat flour prior to cooking – either avoid dusting foods altogether or use naturally gluten-free flours like maize meal or rice flour.

● Potato flour is useful for thickening gravies, stews, casseroles, sauces and soups.

● Roll gluten-free pastry out on greaseproof paper as this makes it easier to lift and to line the tin.

● If gluten-free pastry is very crumbly, press it over the base and up the sides of the tin (as when making shortbread) rather than trying to roll it out.

● Grease baking tins before use, even if they are non-stick, or line the tins with non-stick baking paper to prevent sticking.

● It is a good idea to bake a batch of gluten-free breads, cakes and biscuits and pop some of them into the freezer. Gluten-free baked goods freeze well and will keep fresh for many weeks. Freeze in portions, so that you can thaw exactly what you need for a packed lunch or tea-time treat.

## STORE CUPBOARD ESSENTIALS

Pack your pantry with these items and you'll always have the makings of a gluten-free meal:

● Gluten-free cornflakes, rice crispies, puffed rice cereal.

● Fish, such as anchovies, sardines or tuna, canned in oil, brine or water.

● Canned cooked meat, such as ham or gluten-free corned beef.

● Vegetables canned in water, brine or juice, pickled vegetables.

● Dried vegetables and pulses, plain potato crisps.

● Canned fruit in syrup or juice.

● Plain dried fruit, glacé cherries.

● Fruit juices and squashes (except barley water).

● Rice; also rice noodles and other gluten-free pastas.

● Plain nuts (not dry roasted) and seeds, pure peanut butter.

● Sugars, pure syrups, pure honey, jam, marmalade.

● Dried plain milk, evaporated and condensed milk, tea, pure coffee, good quality plain chocolate.

● Naturally gluten-free flours, including rice flour, gluten-free cornflour, maize flour or maize meal, potato flour and soya flour; also yeast.

● Ground rice, tapioca, buckwheat flakes, millet flakes, rice flakes.

● Gelatine or agar agar.

● Pure vegetable oils, wine vinegar or cider vinegar.

● Salt, black peppercorns, dried herbs, pure spices.

● Pure food flavourings and colourings.

● Tomato purée, garlic purée, gluten-free soy sauce.

*Above: Essential items for your store cupboard should include: rice cakes, polenta, pure spices, dried herbs, gluten-free cornflour, rice noodles, rice and gluten-free flour.*

*Left: Stock-up on naturally gluten-free foods, such as jams and marmalades, canned fruits and vegetables, pickled onions, crisps, dried fruit and gluten-free breakfast cereals.*

# GLUTEN-FREE ACCOMPANIMENTS

Potatoes and rice are particularly good sources of natural, gluten-free carbohydrate. They make ideal accompaniments to many dishes and can be served in a wide variety of ways. Explore the potential of gluten-free pastas, too. Rice noodles and corn pasta are delicious, and polenta is marvellous with sauced dishes; try it freshly cooked or cooled, cut into wedges and shallow fried.

## POTATOES

There are few vegetables as versatile as potatoes. Tiny new potatoes are delicious boiled or steamed, baked potatoes make a meal in themselves with a tasty topping, and home-made chips are one treat a gluten-free diet doesn't deny you. Patties, cakes or croquettes, rolled in crushed gluten-free cornflakes or breadcrumbs, make an excellent accompaniment, and mashed potatoes can be served in numerous ways. Always use the right variety of potato for the job. Scrub potatoes and leave the skins on when roasting or making chips for extra texture, flavour and fibre. For a tasty change, try either sweet potatoes or yams.

## RICE

There are many different varieties of rice including brown and white, long grain, short grain, pudding rice, basmati and risotto rice (arborio), all of which are gluten-free, as is wild rice. Boiled rice can be served as it is, stir-fried or used as the basis for a salad.

*Below: Don't just opt for plain boiled long grain rice, try cooking wild rice, wholegrain rice or risotto rice, for a change.*

*Above: Potatoes, sweet potatoes and yams are all naturally gluten-free.*

## RICE NOODLES

These are made from ground rice and water and range in thickness from very thin to wide ribbons and sheets. They are available fresh or dried and are often soaked in warm water before being briefly cooked.

## CORN PASTA

Pure corn pasta – made from maize without added binders or starch – is ideal for a gluten-free diet. It comes in a variety of flavours (including parsley, spinach and chilli) and in shapes that range from spaghetti to twists and shells. All versions look pretty on the plate and have a good flavour. Corn pasta makes an excellent alternative to durum wheat pasta.

*Above: Corn pasta, rice noodles and polenta make marvellous accompaniments.*

## POLENTA

Coarsely ground maize, this is a staple food in Italy, where it is often served as an accompaniment instead of rice or pasta. The partly cooked ground grain is whisked into boiling water or stock.

## HOW TO COOK POLENTA

Bring 1.2 litres/2 pints/5 cups salted water or stock to the boil in a large saucepan. Sprinkle 175g/6oz/generous 1 cup polenta into the boiling water, stirring continuously. Cook, uncovered, over a very low heat for about 40 minutes, stirring frequently, until cooked and thick. Season and add flavourings, such as cheese, butter, garlic and herbs. Serve hot.

## HOW TO COOK BROWN RICE

Bring 1.4 litres/2¼ pints/5⅔ cups lightly salted water to the boil in a large saucepan. Add 250g/9oz/ 1¼ cups brown rice. Bring back to the boil, then lower the heat and simmer, uncovered, for 25–35 minutes until the rice is tender but retains a bit of bite. Drain the rice in a sieve, rinse with boiling water, then drain thoroughly again.

## HOW TO COOK RICE NOODLES

Bring 2 litres/4½ pints/8 cups lightly salted water to the boil in a large saucepan. Turn off the heat and add 250g/9oz/2¼ cups rice noodles. Stir the noodles with a fork to separate them, cover and set aside for 4 minutes. Drain and serve. If serving the noodles cold, rinse in cold water and drain again.

## GLUTEN-FREE SNACKS AND FINGER FOODS

We all enjoy snacks at some time, particularly when the munchies strike. When baking, make extra gluten-free cakes and biscuits and freeze the surplus in slices. That way, you can thaw individual portions as needed. Occasional treats, such as a bar of gluten-free chocolate or a packet of plain crisps, won't do any harm, but it is useful to have a good selection of healthy and delicious gluten-free snacks and treats available, ready to keep hunger pangs at bay.

● Fresh fruit, such as apples, pears, mangoes, kiwi fruit, pineapple wedges, peaches, apricots and oranges.

● Ready-to-eat dried fruit, such as apricots, peaches, pears, apples, prunes or dried fruit salad.

● Gluten-free crackers, crispbreads and rice cakes. Serve them with plain cheese, such as Cheddar, Red Leicester, Stilton or Emmental.

● Wedges of gluten-free fruit cake.

● Plain nuts, such as walnuts, almonds or hazelnuts or a mixture of nuts and dried fruit, mixed seeds or a mixture of mixed seeds and plain nuts.

● Plain yogurt to which you can add chopped fresh fruit for a sweet treat, or finely diced cucumber and a trace of

*Above: Healthy gluten-free snacks include nuts, mixed nuts and raisins, cheese and rice crackers, and raw vegetable crudités.*

crushed garlic for a savoury surprise; also plain or flavoured fromage frais and gluten-free fruit yogurts.

# CHILDREN AND COELIAC DISEASE

Children diagnosed as having coeliac disease can be treated exactly like their peers in all ways but one; they will have to avoid foods containing gluten for the rest of their lives, but as we have already seen, this is not particularly difficult and will have positive results in terms of health.

If parents treat the situation in a calm, matter-of-fact way, explaining to the child why there are some foods that he or she cannot eat, but not making such an issue of it that the child feels either anxious or isolated, then their son or daughter will rapidly come to terms with the coeliac condition, will adapt to the diet (especially if what's on the menu looks and tastes virtually the same as whatever other children are eating) and will be able to enjoy life to the full.

It is a good idea to avoid giving any child foods containing gluten until they are at least six months old. The child with coeliac disease will thrive during this time. Only when gluten is introduced into the diet – probably as porridge or baby rusks – will the coeliac child develop problems. If this should happen, it is important to see your doctor without delay. Don't change the child's diet in the meanwhile, as this might make the condition more difficult to diagnose.

On diagnosis, you will doubtless be given advice about what to feed your baby. Mashed banana or cooked apple, vegetable purée, puréed steamed fish or chicken, plain natural yogurt – these are standard baby foods – and when you make them yourself you can control the ingredients absolutely.

As your baby grows, you can begin introducing him or her to a wide range of gluten-free foods.

Family, friends and anyone who cares for the child should be told about the coeliac condition (preferably not in front of the child) so that they will not inadvertently offer foods that contain gluten.

It is easier for the coeliac child – and simpler in terms of cooking – if all members of the immediate family eat the same gluten-free foods at mealtimes. When your son or daughter starts playgroup or nursery, explain to the organizer about the coeliac condition and pack gluten-free snacks for playtime. Moulding play dough is a favourite pastime for young children, and parents should be aware that this product does contain wheat flour – just in case the child decides to put it in his mouth, as many young children do.

### SCHOOL DAYS

When your child starts school, it is wise to let the staff know about the condition and explain what it entails. In the case of school dinners, it is advisable to liaise with the teacher or school cook: some school dinners will be naturally gluten-free, and the child who chooses sensibly (under supervision) will be able to enjoy a school

*Left: Playing with play dough is a favourite pastime for young children, but be aware that this product contains wheat flour.*

*Above: When your child starts school, make sure that their teacher is aware of the child's condition and what it entails*

dinner with his friends. Alternatively, your son or daughter could take a gluten-free packed lunch. Most primary schools set aside a special area so that children who have brought their own food can eat together, so this can be just as sociable – just make sure your child knows not to swap!

Invitations to other children's parties won't pose problems if you ring the hosts beforehand and explain the situation. It is easiest if the coeliac child takes his or her own gluten-free food; try to find out what is likely to be on the menu, so that you can send along something that is broadly similar. The child will soon get used to taking his or her own food to parties, and will learn which familar foods are gluten-free and thus okay to eat.

If the party is your own, simply serve gluten-free food for everyone. This is by no means second best: as the recipes in this book prove, gluten-free food can be every bit as delicious as the alternatives.

There is bound to be a time when your child accidentally eats something containing gluten. Don't panic – these mishaps will cause minor upsets, but as long as the child continues on a gluten-free diet, the symptoms will pass in a few days.

If your child is ill, it is equally important not to assume automatically that he or she has eaten something containing gluten; coeliac children succumb to tummy bugs, just like everyone else.

As coeliac children get older, particularly in their teenage years, they like to be one of the crowd and don't wish to be seen as different or an outsider. This is an important time for parents to be supportive and encourage the child to continue following a gluten-free diet.

---

### CHILDREN'S PACKED LUNCHES

- Gluten-free mini scones, muffins or meringues.
- Small packets or bags of dried fruit, such as raisins, ready-to-eat dried apricots, mango, pears, peaches or apples, or mixed dried fruit or prunes.
- Gluten-free snacks, such as plain potato crisps and plain mixed nuts or nuts and raisins (avoid dry-roasted nuts, which may contain gluten).
- Raw carrot or cucumber sticks.
- Rice salad, gluten-free pasta salad, tuna and bean salad, potato salad, other home-made mixed salads.
- Home-made gluten-free soups.
- Cold potatoes with or without a gluten-free dressing.
- Hard-boiled eggs.
- Fresh fruit, such as apples, pears, bananas, oranges, satsumas, clementines, kiwi fruit, cherries, grapes.
- Fresh fruit salad.
- Fresh fruit jelly (set in small covered pot).
- Plain or fruit-flavoured fromage frais, natural yogurts (to which you can add your own choice of chopped fresh fruits) or pure fruit-flavoured yogurts.
- Drinks suitable for packed lunches include fruit squashes, diluted unsweetened fruit juices, milk, home-made milk shakes and water.

---

*Below: Fresh and dried fruits, nuts, yogurt, carrot sticks and crisps are easy to pack into a lunch box. If the school doesn't provide a drink, then include a carton of fresh fruit juice, pure, clear squash, or a small bottle of mineral water, too*

**COOKING FOR A COELIAC CHILD**
Make the menu as varied as possible and be sure to include typical favourites like pizzas (gluten-free), hamburgers and sausages. Bought burgers and sausages often contain rusk or breadcrumbs, so make your own gluten-free alternatives.

Packed lunches should be as colourful and as interesting as you can make them. Sandwiches, baps or rolls made from gluten-free breads are always popular. Try Rice, Buckwheat and Corn Bread or Cheese and Onion Cornbread, add your child's favourite gluten-free filling and you have the perfect finger food. For more packed lunch suggestions, see the list above. If you include salads or desserts, use small pots with good seals and remember to pack a fork or spoon. A small flask is ideal for transporting hot soup or a cold drink.

Don't forget the treats: meringues may not do your child's teeth much good, but they'll do wonders for his or her street cred!

# ENTERTAINING

Sharing food with friends is one of life's great pleasures, whether this consists of a family gathering, a casual supper or a sophisticated dinner party. What we serve depends on the occasion and the appetites and tastes of our guests, but the menu should be planned with an eye to colour, complementary flavours and contrasting textures. It is important to be aware of any special dietary needs – not just those of the coeliac in the family – so that these can be accommodated in such a way that nobody feels singled out. Serving gluten-free food to everyone is the easiest option. This will not pose any particular problems, as the range of healthy, nutritious dishes available is so varied and interesting, and it will be easy to incorporate choices for vegetarian or diabetic guests. On the next few pages you will find menu suggestions for all kinds of occasions.

## GLUTEN-FREE FOOD FOR GROWN-UP GUESTS

Cooking for adults implies a certain sophistication, although this is not necessarily the case, as anyone who has catered to the man or woman who always insists on meat and two veg will appreciate. As a rule, however, grown-ups will eagerly try something new and exciting. They will enjoy sampling rolls, pancakes or pastries made from unfamiliar grains and will be keen to taste your home-made ice cream. Many of your favourite dishes will be naturally gluten-free, and others can easily be adapted.

Note: Where specific dishes are listed, the recipes can be found in the recipe section of the book.

### MENU 1

Prosciutto and Olive Bruschetta
Warm Chicken Salad with
Hazelnut Dressing
or Spicy Carrot Soup with
Croûtons
Baked Trout with Wild
Mushrooms with sautéed
potatoes, steamed green beans,
braised carrots
or Pancetta and Broad Bean
Risotto with mixed green salad
Rich Chocolate Mousse with
Glazed Kumquats
Summer Strawberry Roulade
Selection of red and white wines,
mineral water

### MENU 2

Vegetable crudités and plain crisps
with dips, such as yogurt and
chive, garlic and chilli tomato,
curried gluten-free mayonnaise
Grilled Vegetable Pizza
Tuna, Courgette and
Pepper Frittata
Wild Mushroom and
Broccoli Flan
Thai Chicken and
Vegetable Curry
Lemon Cheesecake with
Forest Fruits
Chocolate Meringues with Mixed
Fruit Compote
Selection of beers, wines, water

## CHOICES FOR CHILDREN'S BIRTHDAY PARTIES

Children love birthday parties. No matter how appealing the package offered by the local pizza parlour or hamburger restaurant, most children would just as soon celebrate at home with presents, party games and a colourful spread with plenty of choice. When giving a party for your coeliac child, avoid complications by making sure that all the food is gluten-free. You don't need to provide a vast amount – most children pick, mix and nibble – but it is important that the eats include plenty of any sweet and savoury treats currently popular on the peer-group party circuit.

### MENU 3

Mini chicken satés
Cheese cubes and pineapple
chunks on cocktail sticks
Grilled bacon and banana rolls
Baked potato skins with a variety
of home-made dips, such as herb
or garlic soured cream, home-
made Thousand Island, fresh
tomato salsa
Chocolate Chip Cookies
Chocolate-dipped strawberries
and grapes
Strawberry yogurt fool
Home-made gluten-free novelty
birthday cake
Fruit juice, water, fruit squashes

### MENU 4

Party sandwiches made using
gluten-free bread with a variety of
gluten-free fillings, such as tuna
and gluten-free mayonnaise, egg
and cress, ham and tomato, cheese
and cucumber
Spiced chicken drumsticks
Plain potato crisps
Sultana and Cinnamon
Chewy Bars
Chocolate rice crispie cakes
Jelly and home-made ice cream
Mini fruit kebabs
Home-made gluten-free novelty
birthday cake
Home-made thick fruit milk shakes

# FAMILY MEALS

Cooking for the family can be satisfying and fun, but it can easily turn into a boring chore. The very fact that you have to do it every day makes it easy to slip into the habit of serving the same old thing week in and week out. When you are catering for a coeliac, there's a particular danger of sticking to a few tried and tested gluten-free dishes. You probably promise yourself that you'll extend your recipe repertoire one day – but you never seem to have the time. That's why we've listed some simple suggestions for gluten-free main courses and puddings, with minimum preparation and maximum family appeal. Use them in addition to the full-scale recipes that follow.

## QUICK AND EASY GLUTEN-FREE MAIN COURSES

● Cook corn pasta, toss in olive oil and add a scattering of Parmesan cheese shavings.

● Chargrill chicken breasts and serve with a tomato and basil salsa (*right*).

● Pan-fry thick cod or salmon steaks in butter and olive oil; add plenty of chopped herbs and a squeeze of lime juice just before serving with roast Mediterranean vegetables.

● Skewer lean lamb, chunks of pepper and thin wedges of red onion on to kebab sticks, baste with olive oil and ground cumin and grill until cooked and golden brown.

● Cook polenta, spoon it around the outside of a serving platter and fill the centre with ratatouille. Offer freshly grated Parmesan separately.

● Marinate strips of pork fillet in a mixture of gluten-free soy sauce, brown sugar and dry sherry. Stir-fry with mangetouts, mushrooms, spring onions, carrot and celery. Serve over rice noodles.

## INSTANT IDEAS FOR GLUTEN-FREE DESSERTS

● Fill a meringue basket with fresh raspberries and top with a spoonful of Greek-style yogurt.

● Pan-fry canned or fresh pineapple slices in a little butter (add a scant sprinkling of brown sugar if you like) and serve with scoops of home-made vanilla ice cream.

● Serve fresh fruits with a dollop of crème fraîche (*left*).

● Make sundaes by layering fresh prepared summer fruits and slices of banana in tall glasses. Drizzle a little orange liqueur over adult portions. Top with dairy cream or crème fraîche.

● Spear fruit, such as melon balls, strawberries, chunks of kiwi fruit and seedless grapes on small wooden skewers. Serve with a dip made from Greek-style yogurt and honey.

● Cook dried fruit salad (or a mixture of prunes, dried apricots or pears and raisins) in a light syrup. Set aside until quite cold, then add blanched almonds and shelled pistachios. Serve with crème fraîche or dairy cream.

● Fill the centre of cored baking apples with chopped dates or mixed dried fruit. Microwave or bake until tender, then drizzle with pure maple syrup and serve solo or with single dairy cream.

# EATING OUT

Some coeliacs are wary of accepting dinner-party invitations, even though they manage their own diet perfectly well at home. They are not alone in this; anyone on a restricted diet is likely to have similar reservations. The simple solution is to ring your host, tell him or her about your condition and explain what you are able to eat. Given due warning, most people will be happy to work out a suitable menu and may even relish the challenge.

When eating out in a restaurant, ask the chef if any dishes are gluten-free, or call ahead to check that they can cater for a coeliac. To be on the safe side, always choose foods that you know to be completely gluten-free.

## DISHES TO CHOOSE

**STARTERS:** Melon, grapefruit, mixed fruit cocktail, melon with Parma ham.

**MAIN COURSES:** Plain grilled or roast meat or fish served without stuffing, sauce or gravy; plain shellfish or seafood; plain meat and vegetable kebabs; plain cold meat or cheese platters; rice dishes, such as risotto or kedgeree; plain or soufflé omelettes.

**ACCOMPANIMENTS:** Salads without dressings, new potatoes or baked potatoes with gluten-free toppings, rice, plain cooked vegetables.

**DESSERTS:** Plain fresh fruit or fruit salad served with natural yogurt or dairy cream, meringues or fresh fruit pavlova, plain grilled, poached or stewed fruit, plain cheeses with fruit.

*When eating out, foods, such as chicken Kiev (above right), which are coated in breadcrumbs, must be avoided, while melon, served with Parma ham (below) makes a safe – and delicious – choice for a starter.*

## DISHES TO AVOID

**STARTERS:** Soups, pâtés, terrines, savoury mousses, any dish served with a dressing, such as mayonnaise or a thickened sauce or gravy.

**MAIN COURSES:** Meat, poultry or fish served with a crumb, batter or oatmeal coating or which may have been coated in flour before being fried; sausages; meat patties; roast meat with stuffing or gravy; stews or casseroles; pies; pizzas, curries; pasta dishes.

**DESSERTS:** Pancakes or crêpes; custards, ice cream and ice cream wafers; baked puddings, such as sponge pudding; cheesecakes; sweet pies and tarts; petits fours; confectionery.

**DRINKS TO AVOID:** Beer, lager, ale and stout; tomato juice (catering packs may contain gluten); drinking chocolate (primarily from vending machines); malted drinks; malted drinking chocolate; malted milk drinks.

**DRINKS TO CHOOSE:** Wine, champagne, cider, spirits, such as sherry, whisky and brandy, fruit squashes (except barley water), fruit juices, tea, pure coffee (not instant). Soft drinks and most fizzy drinks are gluten-free, but avoid any that are cloudy, as these may contain starch.

*Below: To accompany your meal, choose alcoholic drinks, such as red and white wine and champagne or spirit-based drinks, such as gin and tonic, or stick to clear fizzy drinks, fresh fruit juice – or water.*

### SAFE SEASONING

In restaurants and canteens, avoid seasoning food with ground white pepper – many caterers "stretch" the pepper by adding wheat flour. To be safe, ask for the pepper mill and grind black pepper directly on to your food.

## PICNICS

Picnics provide the perfect opportunity for families and friends to get together. Whether you pack a simple selection of gluten-free sandwiches and snacks, or go all out with an impressive assortment of sweet and savoury dishes, there's something special about eating *al fresco*.

Picnic foods should be fairly easy to carry, quick to serve and easy to eat. Many dishes can be prepared up to a day in advance and kept chilled until ready to transport.

For a simple picnic, serve a selection of plain cold meats and cheeses, with rice bread or a similar gluten-free loaf. Celery sticks, cherry tomatoes and a simple green salad complete the spread, with a gluten-free vinaigrette dressing in a tightly sealed plastic container. Fresh fruit makes the perfect finale.

For a slightly more extravagant picnic, add some dishes from the column on the right. The picnic basket might also contain a selection of salads with suitable dressings (tomato salad with basil and mozzarella; new potatoes with gluten-free herb vinaigrette; French bean salad with almonds) and some gluten-free pâtés. If you pack pickles and chutneys, make sure they are home-made as some commercial products contain gluten. A big bowl of strawberries or raspberries will make a delicious dessert with tiny meringues and a bowl of dairy cream. Pack plenty of drinks – and don't forget paper napkins, wet wipes and bags for the disposal of any rubbish.

*Below: Family picnic foods need to be simple and fairly easy to carry – fresh fruit makes the perfect, gluten-free finale.*

### GLUTEN-FREE PICNIC FOODS

Where specific dishes are listed, the recipes can be found in the recipe section of the book.

● Spiced chicken drumsticks or chicken wings.

● Gluten-free pizza, such as Grilled Vegetable Pizza.

● Crudités, such as carrot and cucumber sticks or batons; cauliflower and broccoli florets; lettuce hearts; courgette, pepper and fennel sticks; cherry tomatoes; radishes and celery sticks, served with a gluten-free dip, such as natural yogurt mixed with finely diced cucumber, chopped fresh mint or parsley and crushed garlic.

● Wild Mushroom and Broccoli Flan or a similar gluten-free quiche or savoury tart.

● Savoury Nut Loaf.

● Various salads, including Mixed Leaf and Herb Salad, Rice Salad, Gluten-free Pasta Salad, Potato Salad, Three Bean Salad, Fruit and Nut Coleslaw.

● Gluten-free breads: Rice, Buckwheat and Corn Bread, Cheese and Onion Cornbread.

● Desserts, such as fresh fruit salad or Summer Fruit Roulade.

● Apple and Orange Muffins, Cinnamon Chewy Bars, Chocolate Chip Cookies, Cherry Coconut Munchies.

● Victoria Sandwich Cake, Fruit, Nut and Seed Loaf, Gingerbread, Country Apple Cake.

# BASIC RECIPES

There is a wide range of stock products on the market including cubes of various flavours, stock powders or granules and fresh chilled stock, but some of these contain gluten, so it is worth-while making your own gluten-free stocks at home. Home-made stocks add delicious flavour to many different dishes, and they really are simple to make. It is a good idea to prepare one or two batches and freeze them in useful quantities for future use. Cool home-made stocks quickly, pour them into suitable containers (leaving space for expansion) and freeze them for up to 3 months.

---

### CHICKEN STOCK
*Makes about 750ml/1¼ pints/3 cups*
1 meaty chicken carcass
6 shallots or 1 onion
1 carrot
2 celery sticks
1 bay leaf
salt and ground black pepper

*1* Break or chop the chicken carcass into pieces and place in a large saucepan with 1.75 litres/3 pints/7½ cups cold water.

*2* Peel and slice the shallots or onion and carrot, then chop the celery. Add the vegetables to the saucepan with the bayleaf. Stir to mix.

*3* Bring to the boil, then partially cover and simmer for 2 hours, skimming off any scum and fat that rises to the surface during cooking.

*4* Strain the stock through a sieve, then set aside to cool.

*5* When cold, remove and discard all the fat and use the stock or freeze. Once cool, cover and store in the fridge for up to 3 days. Season with salt and pepper, as required.

### BEEF STOCK
*Makes about 750ml/1¼ pints/3 cups*
450g/1lb shin of beef on the bone
450g/1lb beef or veal bones
1 onion
1 carrot
1 turnip
2 celery sticks
1 leek
1 bouquet garni
salt and ground black pepper

*1* Preheat the oven to 220°C/425°F/ Gas 7. Place the meat and bones in a roasting tin and brown in the oven for about 30 minutes, then place in a large pan with 1.75 litres/3 pints/ 7½ cups cold water.

*2* Peel and slice the onion and carrot, then peel and dice the turnip and chop the celery and leek. Add the vegetables to the saucepan with the bouquet garni. Stir to mix.

*3* Bring to the boil, then partially cover and simmer for 2 hours, skimming off any scum and fat that rises to the surface during cooking. Strain the stock through a fine sieve, then set aside to cool. Store as for chicken stock.

### VEGETABLE STOCK
*Makes about 1.5 litres/2½ pints/6¼ cups*
1 large onion, sliced
2 carrots, sliced
1 leek, sliced
3 celery sticks, chopped
1 small turnip, diced
1 small parsnip, sliced
1 bouquet garni
salt and ground black pepper

*1* Place all the prepared vegetables in a large saucepan with the bouquet garni. Add 1.75 litres/3 pints/7½ cups cold water and stir to mix.

*2* Bring to the boil, then partially cover and simmer for about 1 hour, skimming off any scum.

*3* Strain the stock through a sieve, use immediately or set aside to cool. Store in the fridge for up to 3 days. Alternatively, freeze the stock. Season with salt and pepper, as required.

### COOK'S TIP
If you have any vegetable trimmings, such as tomato or onion skins, celery tops or cabbage leaves, then add these to the water with the vegetables when making the stock.

### GLUTEN-FREE WHITE SAUCE

*Makes about 300ml/1/2 pint/1 1/4 cups*
30ml/2 tbsp gluten-free cornflour
300ml/1/2 pint/1 1/4 cups semi-
  skimmed milk
15g/1/2oz/1 tbsp sunflower
  margarine
salt and ground black pepper

*1* Place the cornflour in a bowl and
blend with 60ml/4 tbsp of the milk
to make a smooth paste.

*2* Heat the remaining milk in a
saucepan over a medium heat until
boiling, then pour on to the blended
mixture, whisking continuously to
prevent lumps forming.

*3* Return the mixture to the
saucepan and bring slowly to the
boil, stirring continuously, until the
sauce thickens. Lower the heat and
simmer gently for 2–3 minutes, then
stir in the margarine, until melted.
Season to taste and serve.

### VARIATIONS

To make a thinner pouring sauce,
reduce the quantity of cornflour to
20–25ml/4–5 tsp.

Replace half the milk with well-
flavoured vegetable or chicken stock or
use a half-and-half mixture of stock
and white wine in place of the milk.

Add gluten-free flavourings, such as
grated cheese, chopped mixed fresh
herbs, lightly sautéed onions, tomato
purée, or chopped or sliced, cooked
wild or button mushrooms, to the
sauce for extra flavour.

### FRENCH DRESSING

*Makes about 150ml/1/4 pint/2/3 cup*
90ml/6 tbsp olive or sunflower oil
30ml/2 tbsp white wine vinegar or
  lemon juice
5ml/1 tsp Dijon mustard
1.5ml/1/4 tsp caster sugar
15ml/1 tbsp chopped fresh
  mixed herbs
salt and ground black pepper

*1* Place all the ingredients in a small
bowl and whisk together until
thoroughly mixed. Alternatively, place
all the ingredients in a clean, screw-
top jar, seal and shake well until
thoroughly mixed.

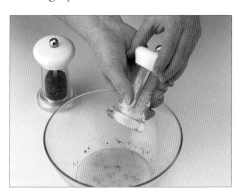

*2* Adjust the seasoning and serve
immediately or keep in a screw-top
jar in the fridge for up to 1 week.
Shake thoroughly before serving.

### VARIATION

Crush a small garlic clove and add to
the dressing, if liked.

### MAYONNAISE

*Makes about 200ml/7fl oz/scant 1 cup*
2 egg yolks
5ml/1 tsp Dijon mustard
15ml/1 tbsp lemon juice
2.5ml/1/2 tsp salt
ground black pepper
about 150ml/1/4 pint/2/3 cup olive or
  sunflower oil

*1* Place the egg yolks, mustard,
lemon juice, salt, pepper and
15ml/1 tbsp oil in a small blender or
food processor. Blend for 30 seconds.

*2* With the motor running, gradually
add the remaining oil, pouring it
through the funnel in a slow, contin-
uous stream, until the mayonnaise is
thick, creamy and smooth.

*3* Adjust the seasoning, then use
immediately or cover and chill
until required. Store for up to 3 days in
a covered container in the fridge.

### VARIATIONS

Add finely chopped garlic, capers,
gherkins or cucumber, crumbled blue
cheese or chopped fresh mixed herbs.

# SOUPS, SNACKS AND SALADS

*If you enjoy a steaming bowl of hot soup, served with home-made gluten-free bread, or a quick light salad or tasty snack for lunch or supper, you will find a tempting selection of recipes in this chapter. Try, for example, Spicy Carrot Soup with Garlic Croûtons, Grilled Vegetable Pizza, Bacon and Herb Rösti or Warm Chicken Salad with Hazelnut Dressing.*

# Spicy Carrot Soup with Garlic Croûtons

## INGREDIENTS

*Serves 6*
15ml/1 tbsp olive oil
1 large onion, chopped
675g/1½lb carrots, sliced
5ml/1 tsp each ground coriander,
 ground cumin and hot chilli powder
900ml/1½ pints/3¾ cups vegetable or
 chicken stock
salt and ground black pepper
fresh coriander sprigs, to garnish

**For the garlic croûtons**
a little olive oil, for frying
2 garlic cloves, crushed
4 slices of gluten-free bread, crusts
 removed, cut into 1cm/½in cubes

*1* To make the soup, heat the oil in a
 large saucepan, add the onion and
carrots and cook gently for 5 minutes,
stirring occasionally. Add the ground
spices and cook gently for 1 minute,
continuing to stir.

*2* Stir in the stock, bring to the boil,
 then cover and cook gently for
about 45 minutes until the carrots are
tender, stirring occasionally.

*3* Meanwhile, make the garlic
 croûtons. Heat a little oil in a
frying pan, add the garlic and cook
gently for 30 seconds, stirring. Add the
bread cubes, turn them over in the oil
and fry over a medium heat for a few
minutes until crisp and golden brown
all over, turning frequently. Drain on
kitchen paper and keep warm.

*4* Purée the soup in a blender or food
 processor until smooth, then season
to taste with salt and pepper. Return
the soup to the rinsed-out saucepan
and reheat gently. Serve hot, sprinkled
with garlic croûtons and garnished with
coriander sprigs.

| — NUTRITION NOTES — | |
|---|---|
| Per portion: | |
| Energy | 127kcals/529kJ |
| Fat, total | 6.1g |
| saturated fat | 0.92g |
| Protein | 2.65g |
| Carbohydrate | 17.2g |
| sugar, total | 7.74g |
| Fibre – NSP | 2.94g |
| Sodium | 626mg |

---

# Sweet Potato and Parsnip Soup

## INGREDIENTS

*Serves 6*
15ml/1 tbsp sunflower oil
1 large leek, sliced
2 celery sticks, chopped
450g/1lb sweet potatoes, diced
225g/8oz parsnips, diced
900ml/1½ pints/3¾ cups vegetable or
 chicken stock
salt and ground black pepper
15ml/1 tbsp chopped fresh parsley and
 roasted strips of sweet potatoes and
 parsnips, to garnish

*1* Heat the oil in a large saucepan,
 add the leek, celery, sweet potatoes
and parsnips. Cook gently for about
5 minutes, stirring to prevent them
browning or sticking to the pan.

*2* Stir in the vegetable or chicken
 stock and bring to the boil, then
cover and simmer gently for about
25 minutes, or until the vegetables are
tender, stirring occasionally. Season to
taste with salt and pepper.

*3* Remove the pan from the heat and
 allow to cool slightly.

*4* Purée the soup in a blender or food
 processor until smooth, then return
the soup to the saucepan and reheat
gently. Ladle into warmed soup bowls
to serve and sprinkle over the chopped
fresh parsley and roasted strips of sweet
potatoes and parsnips to garnish.

| — NUTRITION NOTES — | |
|---|---|
| Per portion: | |
| Energy | 115kcals/486kJ |
| Fat, total | 4g |
| saturated fat | 0.46g |
| Protein | 3.1g |
| Carbohydrate | 17.9g |
| sugar, total | 3.72g |
| Fibre – NSP | 3.07g |
| Sodium | 780mg |

# Fresh Mushroom Soup with Tarragon

This is a light mushroom soup subtly flavoured with tarragon.

## INGREDIENTS

*Serves 6*
15g/½oz/1 tbsp sunflower margarine
4 shallots, finely chopped
450g/1lb chestnut mushrooms,
    finely chopped
300ml/½ pint/1¼ cups vegetable stock
300ml/½ pint/1¼ cups semi-
    skimmed milk
15–30ml/1–2 tbsp chopped
    fresh tarragon
30ml/2 tbsp dry sherry (optional)
salt and ground black pepper
fresh tarragon sprigs, to garnish

---
VARIATION

---

Use a mixture of wild and button mushrooms instead of chestnut mushrooms.

*1* Melt the margarine in a large saucepan, add the shallots and cook gently for 5 minutes, stirring them occasionally. Add the mushrooms and cook gently for 3 minutes, stirring.

*2* Stir in the stock and milk, bring to the boil, then cover and simmer gently for about 20 minutes until the vegetables are soft. Stir in the chopped tarragon and season to taste with salt and pepper.

*3* Allow the soup to cool slightly, then purée in a blender or food processor, in batches if necessary until smooth. Return to the rinsed-out saucepan and reheat gently.

*4* Stir in the sherry, if using, then ladle the soup into warmed soup bowls and serve garnished with tarragon sprigs.

--- NUTRITION NOTES ---

Per portion:

| | |
|---|---|
| Energy | 65kcals/275kJ |
| Fat, total | 3.5g |
| saturated fat | 1.2g |
| Protein | 3.6g |
| Carbohydrate | 3.9g |
| sugar, total | 3.3g |
| Fibre – NSP | 1g |
| Sodium | 250mg |

# Prosciutto and Olive Bruschetta

A classic Italian snack, these appetizing toasts are ideal either on their own as finger food or as a starter served with a lightly dressed mixed leaf salad and accompanied by a glass of chilled white wine.

## INGREDIENTS

*Serves 4*
4 slices of gluten-free bread
1 whole garlic clove, halved
a little olive oil, for drizzling
small handful of basil leaves
4 prosciutto slices
50g/2oz/½ cup pitted black olives,
    roughly chopped
grated fresh Parmesan cheese, to
    serve (optional)

*1* Toast the bread lightly on both sides until golden brown.

*2* Cut larger slices of bread in half, if liked, then rub one side of each piece of toast with the cut side of the halved garlic clove.

--- NUTRITION NOTES ---

Per portion:

| | |
|---|---|
| Energy | 176kcals/732kJ |
| Fat, total | 9.1g |
| saturated fat | 3.4g |
| Protein | 9.9g |
| Carbohydrate | 13.7g |
| sugar, total | 1.2g |
| Fibre – NSP | 0.5g |
| Sodium | 703mg |

*3* Drizzle a little olive oil over each slice of toast. Top with some basil leaves, then the slices of prosciutto, arranging the slices to fit the shape of the toast. Scatter the chopped black olives over the top.

*4* Serve the bruschetta immediately, with a little grated Parmesan cheese sprinkled over them, if liked.

# Bacon and Herb Rösti

## INGREDIENTS

### Serves 4

450g/1lb potatoes, left whole
  and unpeeled
30ml/2 tbsp olive oil
1 red onion, finely chopped
4 lean back bacon rashers, rinded
  and diced
15ml/1 tbsp potato flour
30ml/2 tbsp chopped fresh
  mixed herbs
salt and ground black pepper
fresh parsley sprigs, to garnish

*1* Lightly grease a baking sheet. Parboil the potatoes in a saucepan of lightly salted, boiling water for about 6 minutes. Drain the potatoes and set aside to cool slightly.

*2* Once cool enough to handle, peel the potatoes and coarsely grate them into a bowl. Set aside.

*3* Heat 15ml/1 tbsp of the oil in a frying pan, add the onion and bacon and cook gently for 5 minutes, stirring occasionally. Preheat the oven to 220°C/425°F/Gas 7.

*4* Remove the pan from the heat. Stir the onion mixture, remaining oil, potato flour, herbs and seasoning into the grated potatoes and mix well.

*5* Divide the mixture into eight small piles and spoon them on to the prepared baking sheet, leaving a little space between them.

*6* Bake for 20–25 minutes until the rösti are crisp and golden brown. Serve immediately, garnished with sprigs of fresh parsley.

| NUTRITION NOTES | |
|---|---|
| Per portion: | |
| Energy | 245kcals/1025kJ |
| Fat, total | 12.6g |
|   saturated fat | 2.9g |
| Protein | 10.7g |
| Carbohydrate | 23.6g |
|   sugar, total | 1.8g |
| Fibre – NSP | 2.6g |
| Sodium | 572mg |

# *Grilled Vegetable Pizza*

## INGREDIENTS

*Serves 6*

1 courgette, sliced
2 baby aubergines or 1 small
  aubergine, sliced
30ml/2 tbsp olive oil
1 yellow pepper, seeded and
  thickly sliced
115g/4oz/1 cup gluten-free cornmeal
50g/2oz/½ cup potato flour
50g/2oz/½ cup soya flour
5ml/1 tsp gluten-free baking powder
2.5ml/½ tsp salt
50g/2oz/4 tbsp soft margarine
about 105ml/7 tbsp semi-
  skimmed milk
4 plum tomatoes, skinned
  and chopped
30ml/2 tbsp chopped fresh basil
115g/4oz mozzarella cheese, sliced
salt and ground black pepper
fresh basil sprigs, to garnish

*1* Preheat the grill. Brush the
courgette and aubergine slices with
a little oil and place on a grill rack with
the pepper slices. Cook under the grill
until lightly browned, turning once.

*2* Meanwhile, preheat the oven to
200°C/400°F/Gas 6. Place the
cornmeal, potato flour, soya flour,
baking powder and salt in a mixing
bowl and stir to mix. Lightly rub in the
margarine until the mixture resembles
coarse breadcrumbs, then stir in
enough of the milk to make a soft but
not sticky dough.

---- NUTRITION NOTES ----

Per portion:
| | |
|---|---|
| Energy | 326kcals/1362kJ |
| Fat, total | 19.5g |
| saturated fat | 5.8g |
| Protein | 12.2g |
| Carbohydrate | 26.8g |
| sugar, total | 5.1g |
| Fibre – NSP | 3.2g |
| Sodium | 365mg |

*3* Place the dough on a sheet of non-
stick baking paper on a baking
sheet and roll or press it out to form a
25cm/10in round, making the edges
slightly thicker than the centre.

*4* Brush the pizza dough with any
remaining oil, then spread the
chopped tomatoes over the dough.

*5* Sprinkle with the chopped basil
and season with salt and pepper.
Arrange the grilled vegetables over the
tomatoes and top with the cheese.

*6* Bake for 25–30 minutes until crisp
and golden brown. Garnish the
pizza with fresh basil sprigs and serve
immediately, cut into slices.

# Warm Chicken Salad with Hazelnut Dressing

This simple warm salad combines pan-fried chicken and spinach with a light, nutty dressing.

## INGREDIENTS

*Serves 4*
45ml/3 tbsp olive oil
30ml/2 tbsp hazelnut oil
15ml/1 tbsp white wine vinegar
1 garlic clove, crushed
15ml/1 tbsp chopped fresh mixed herbs
225g/8oz baby spinach leaves
250g/9oz cherry tomatoes, halved
1 bunch spring onions, chopped
2 skinless, boneless chicken breasts, cut into thin strips
salt and ground black pepper

---
### VARIATION
---

Use other meat or fish such as beef or salmon in place of the chicken.

*1* First make the dressing, place 30ml/2 tbsp of the olive oil, the hazelnut oil, vinegar, garlic and chopped herbs in a small bowl or jug and whisk together until thoroughly mixed. Set aside.

*2* Trim any long stalks from the spinach leaves, then place in a large serving bowl with the tomatoes and spring onions and toss together to mix.

---
### NUTRITION NOTES
---

| Per portion: | |
| --- | --- |
| Energy | 300kcals/1250kJ |
| Fat, total | 20.9g |
| saturated fat | 2.7g |
| Protein | 23.2g |
| Carbohydrate | 4.8g |
| sugar, total | 4.5g |
| Fibre – NSP | 2.4g |
| Sodium | 126mg |

*3* Heat the remaining 15ml/1 tbsp olive oil in a frying pan, add the chicken and stir-fry over a high heat for 7–10 minutes until the chicken is cooked, tender and lightly browned.

*4* Scatter the cooked chicken pieces over the salad, give the dressing a quick whisk to blend, then drizzle it over the salad and gently toss all the ingredients together to mix. Season to taste with salt and pepper and serve immediately.

---

# Fruit and Nut Coleslaw

A delicious and nutritious mixture of crunchy vegetables, fruit and nuts, tossed together in a light mayonnaise dressing.

## INGREDIENTS

*Serves 6*
225g/8oz white cabbage
1 large carrot
175g/6oz/¾ cup ready-to-eat dried apricots
50g/2oz/½ cup walnuts
50g/2oz/½ cup hazelnuts
115g/4oz/1 cup raisins
30ml/2 tbsp chopped fresh parsley or chives or a mixture
105ml/7 tbsp gluten-free reduced-calorie mayonnaise
75ml/5 tbsp low-fat natural yogurt
salt and ground black pepper
fresh chives, to garnish

*1* Finely shred the cabbage, coarsely grate the carrot and place both in a large mixing bowl. Roughly chop the apricots and nuts. Stir them into the cabbage and carrots with the raisins and chopped herbs.

*2* In a separate bowl, mix together the mayonnaise and yogurt and season to taste with salt and pepper.

*3* Add the mayonnaise to the cabbage mixture and toss together to mix.

*4* Cover the bowl and set aside in a cool place for at least 30 minutes before serving, to allow the flavours to mingle. Serve the coleslaw garnished with a few fresh chives.

---
### NUTRITION NOTES
---

| Per portion: | |
| --- | --- |
| Energy | 283kcals/1185kJ |
| Fat, total | 16.4g |
| saturated fat | 0.9g |
| Protein | 5.5g |
| Carbohydrate | 30.1g |
| sugar, total | 29g |
| Fibre – NSP | 4.4g |
| Sodium | 199mg |

# Seafood and Herb Salad

Quick and easy to prepare, this warm, mixed seafood salad makes a great lunchtime snack. Serve with baked potatoes for a more substantial meal.

## INGREDIENTS

*Serves 4*
30ml/2 tbsp olive oil
15ml/1 tbsp flavoured oil, such as basil oil or chilli oil
finely grated rind of 1 small lemon
15ml/1 tbsp lemon juice
1 garlic clove, crushed
30ml/2 tbsp chopped fresh basil
175g/6oz mixed salad leaves
115g/4oz sugar snap peas, chopped
400g/14oz packet frozen seafood mix, defrosted and drained
salt and ground black pepper

*1* Place 15ml/1 tbsp of the olive oil, the flavoured oil, grated lemon rind, lemon juice, garlic and basil in a small bowl or jug. Season with salt and pepper to taste and whisk together until thoroughly mixed. Set aside.

*2* Place the salad leaves and sugar snap peas in a serving bowl and toss lightly to mix.

*3* Heat the remaining olive oil in a large frying pan or wok, add the seafood and stir-fry over a medium heat for about 5 minutes until cooked. Scatter the seafood over the salad leaves, drizzle the dressing over the salad, toss together to mix and serve.

——— NUTRITION NOTES ———

Per portion:
| | |
|---|---|
| Energy | 202kcals/845kJ |
| Fat, total | 12.8g |
|   saturated fat | 1.8g |
| Protein | 18.1g |
| Carbohydrate | 3.8g |
|   sugar, total | 1.9g |
| Fibre – NSP | 1.1g |
| Sodium | 289mg |

——— VARIATION ———

Use fresh cooked seafood of your choice instead of a ready-mixed packet.

# Citrus Fruit Salad

A refreshingly tangy combination – rocket and lamb's lettuce leaves are topped with fresh grapefruit, oranges and avocado in a light, fruity dressing.

## INGREDIENTS

*Serves 4*
1 pink grapefruit
2 oranges
1 avocado
50g/2oz/½ cup pine nuts
25ml/1½ tbsp olive oil
10ml/2 tsp balsamic vinegar
30ml/2 tbsp freshly squeezed orange juice
50g/2oz lamb's lettuce
50g/2oz rocket
salt and ground black pepper
fresh herb sprigs, to garnish

*1* Halve and segment the grapefruit and oranges and place the segments in a mixing bowl. Squeeze any juices into the bowl, if liked.

*2* Peel and slice the avocado and add the slices to the bowl.

*3* Gently stir in the pine nuts, taking care not to break up the avocado.

*4* Whisk together the olive oil, vinegar, orange juice and seasoning in a small bowl or jug and stir into the fruit mixture. Arrange the lamb's lettuce and rocket on four serving plates and spoon a little fruit and dressing over each. Garnish with herb sprigs and serve immediately.

——— NUTRITION NOTES ———

Per portion:
| | |
|---|---|
| Energy | 307kcals/845kJ |
| Fat, total | 26.6g |
|   saturated fat | 3.56g |
| Protein | 4.8g |
| Carbohydrate | 12.8g |
|   sugar, total | 11.8g |
| Fibre – NSP | 4.95g |
| Sodium | 63mg |

# MEAT, POULTRY AND FISH

*Meat, poultry or fish form the basis of many delicious gluten-free recipes and, when served with cooked potatoes, rice or rice noodles and seasonal fresh vegetables, make tasty, filling and healthy meals. The following tempting selection of recipes, which includes Pancetta and Broad Bean Risotto, Beef and Broccoli Stir-fry, Cod, Tomato and Pepper Bake and Pan-fried Chicken with Pesto, will appeal to the whole family.*

# Pancetta and Broad Bean Risotto

This delicious risotto makes a healthy and filling meal, served with cooked fresh seasonal vegetables or a mixed green salad.

### INGREDIENTS

*Serves 4*
15ml/1 tbsp olive oil
1 onion, chopped
2 garlic cloves, finely chopped
175g/6oz smoked pancetta, diced
350g/12oz/1¾ cups risotto rice
1.2 litres/2 pints/5 cups chicken stock
225g/8oz frozen baby broad beans
30ml/2 tbsp chopped fresh mixed
    herbs, such as parsley, thyme
    and oregano
salt and ground black pepper
shavings of Parmesan cheese, to serve
chopped fresh flat leaf parsley,
    to garnish

*1* Heat the oil in a large saucepan or frying pan. Add the onion, garlic and pancetta and cook gently for about 5 minutes, stirring occasionally.

*2* Add the rice to the pan and cook for 1 minute, stirring. Add 300ml/½ pint/1¼ cups of the stock and simmer, stirring frequently until it has been absorbed.

*3* Continue adding the stock, a ladleful at a time, stirring frequently until the rice is *al dente* and creamy, and almost all the liquid has been absorbed. This will take 30–35 minutes. It may not be necessary to add all the stock.

*4* Meanwhile, cook the broad beans in a saucepan of lightly salted, boiling water for about 3 minutes until tender. Drain and keep warm.

*5* Stir the beans, mixed herbs and seasoning into the risotto. Serve sprinkled with shavings of Parmesan cheese and garnished with parsley.

| NUTRITION NOTES | |
|---|---|
| Per portion: | |
| Energy | 485kcals/2031kJ |
| Fat, total | 9.9g |
| saturated fat | 1.7g |
| Protein | 22.35g |
| Carbohydrate | 74.7g |
| sugar, total | 1.93g |
| Fibre – NSP | 4.36g |
| Sodium | 1969mg |

# Pork Meatballs with Pasta

Serve these tasty meatballs on a bed of freshly cooked gluten-free pasta, such as corn spaghetti.

## INGREDIENTS

*Serves 6*
450g/1lb lean minced pork
1 leek, finely chopped
115g/4oz mushrooms, finely chopped
15ml/1 tbsp chopped fresh thyme
15ml/1 tbsp tomato purée
1 egg, beaten
30ml/2 tbsp potato flour
15ml/1 tbsp sunflower oil
350–500g/12oz–1¼lb gluten-
    free pasta
fresh thyme sprigs, to garnish

**For the tomato sauce**
1 onion, finely chopped
1 carrot, finely chopped
1 celery stick, finely chopped
1 garlic clove, crushed
675g/1½lb ripe tomatoes, skinned,
    seeded and chopped
150ml/¼ pint/⅔ cup dry white wine
150ml/¼ pint/⅔ cup well-flavoured
    vegetable stock
15ml/1 tbsp tomato purée
15ml/1 tbsp chopped fresh basil
salt and ground black pepper

*1* Preheat the oven to 180°C/350°F/ Gas 4. To make the meatballs, put the pork, leek, mushrooms, chopped thyme, tomato purée, egg and potato flour in a bowl and stir together until thoroughly mixed. Shape into small balls, place on a plate, cover and chill while making the tomato sauce.

*2* Place all the sauce ingredients in a small saucepan, season to taste, then bring to the boil. Boil, uncovered, for 10 minutes until thickened.

| NUTRITION NOTES | |
|---|---|
| Per portion: | |
| Energy | 504kcals/2113kJ |
| Fat, total | 8.8g |
| saturated fat | 2.2g |
| Protein | 26.5g |
| Carbohydrate | 76.4g |
| sugar, total | 6.9g |
| Fibre – NSP | 2.5g |
| Sodium | 295mg |

*3* Heat the oil in a frying pan, add the meatballs and cook in batches until lightly browned. Place them in a shallow, ovenproof dish and pour the tomato sauce over. Cover and bake for about 1 hour until cooked through.

*4* Meanwhile, cook the pasta in a pan of lightly salted, boiling water for 8–12 minutes, or according to the packet instructions until *al dente*. Rinse under boiling water and then drain.

*5* Spoon the cooked pasta into warmed bowls, spoon the meatballs and sauce over the top and serve garnished with fresh thyme sprigs.

# Braised Lamb with Apricots and Herb Dumplings

A rich and fruity lamb casserole, topped with light, herby gluten-free dumplings, which is delicious served with baked jacket potatoes and broccoli.

## INGREDIENTS

*Serves 6*

30ml/2 tbsp sunflower oil
675g/1½lb lean lamb fillet, cut into
   2.5cm/1in cubes
350g/12oz button onions, peeled
1 garlic clove, crushed
225g/8oz button mushrooms
175g/6oz/¾ cup small ready-to-eat
   dried apricots
250ml/8fl oz/1 cup well-flavoured
   lamb or beef stock
250ml/8fl oz/1 cup red wine
15ml/1 tbsp tomato purée
salt and ground black pepper
fresh herb sprigs, to garnish

**For the dumplings**
115g/4oz/1 cup gluten-free
   self-raising flour
50g/2oz/scant ½ cup gluten-free
   shredded vegetable suet
15–30ml/1–2 tbsp chopped fresh
   mixed herbs

---
VARIATIONS
---

Use lean beef or pork in place of the lamb and substitute shallots for the button onions, if you prefer.

---
NUTRITION NOTES
---

Per portion:
| | |
|---|---|
| Energy | 513kcals/3204kJ |
| Fat, total | 28.8g |
|   saturated fat | 11.6g |
| Protein | 26.1g |
| Carbohydrate | 31.6g |
|   sugar, total | 15.3g |
| Fibre – NSP | 3.4g |
| Sodium | 257mg |

1 Preheat the oven to 160°C/325°F/ Gas 3. Heat the oil in a large, flameproof casserole, add the lamb and cook gently until browned all over, stirring occasionally. Remove the meat from the casserole using a slotted spoon, set aside and keep warm.

2 Add the button onions, garlic and mushrooms to the oil remaining in the casserole and cook gently for about 5 minutes, stirring occasionally.

3 Return the meat to the casserole, add the dried apricots, stock, wine and tomato purée. Season to taste with salt and pepper and stir to mix.

4 Bring to the boil, stirring, then remove the casserole from the heat and cover. Transfer the casserole to the oven and cook for 1½–2 hours until the lamb is cooked and tender, stirring once or twice and adding a little extra stock, if necessary.

5 Meanwhile, make the dumplings. Place the flour, suet, herbs and seasoning in a bowl and stir to mix. Add enough cold water to make a soft, elastic dough. Divide the dough into small, marble-size pieces and, using lightly floured hands, roll each piece into a small ball.

6 Remove the lid from the casserole and place the dumplings on the top of the braised lamb and vegetables.

7 Increase the oven temperature to 190°C/375°F/Gas 5. Return the casserole to the oven and cook for a further 20–25 minutes until the herb dumplings are cooked. Serve, garnished with fresh herb sprigs.

# Beef and Broccoli Stir-fry

A quick-to-make dish with Oriental appeal.

## INGREDIENTS

*Serves 4*
10ml/2 tsp gluten-free cornflour
45ml/3 tbsp gluten-free soy sauce
45ml/3 tbsp ruby port
15ml/1 tbsp sunflower oil
350g/12oz lean beef steak, cut into
   thin strips
1 garlic clove, crushed
2.5cm/1in piece fresh root ginger,
   peeled and finely chopped
1 red pepper, seeded and sliced
225g/8oz small broccoli florets
salt and ground black pepper
fresh parsley sprigs, to garnish
herby brown rice or rice noodles,
   to serve

*1* Blend the cornflour with the soy sauce and port in a small bowl.

*2* Heat the oil in a large frying pan or wok, add the beef, garlic and ginger and stir-fry over a medium heat for 2–3 minutes until the beef is browned all over. Add the red pepper and broccoli; stir-fry for 4–5 minutes until the vegetables are just tender.

*3* Add the cornflour mixture and salt and pepper to the pan, then cook, stirring all the time until the sauce thickens and becomes glossy. Lower the heat and stir-fry for a further 1 minute. Serve at once, garnished with parsley sprigs and accompanied by herby brown rice or rice noodles.

| ——— NUTRITION NOTES ——— | |
| --- | --- |
| Per portion: | |
| Energy | 217kcals/909kJ |
| Fat, total | 9.8g |
|    saturated fat | 3.0g |
| Protein | 21.9g |
| Carbohydrate | 7.4g |
|    sugar, total | 3.8g |
| Fibre – NSP | 1.86g |
| Sodium | 46mg |

# Pan-fried Chicken with Pesto

Pan-fried chicken, served with warm pesto, makes a deliciously quick main course. Serve with boiled gluten-free pasta or rice noodles and braised vegetables.

## INGREDIENTS

*Serves 4*
15ml/1 tbsp olive oil
4 skinless, boneless chicken breasts
fresh basil leaves, to garnish
braised baby carrots and celery,
   to serve

## For the pesto
90ml/6 tbsp olive oil
50g/2oz/½ cup pine nuts
50g/2oz/⅔ cup freshly grated
   Parmesan cheese
50g/2oz/1 cup fresh basil leaves
15g/½oz/¼ cup fresh parsley
2 garlic cloves, crushed
salt and ground black pepper

*1* Heat the 15ml/1 tbsp oil in a frying pan. Add the chicken breasts and cook gently for 15–20 minutes, turning several times until the chicken breasts are tender, lightly browned and thoroughly cooked.

*2* Meanwhile, make the pesto. Place the olive oil, pine nuts, Parmesan cheese, basil leaves, parsley, garlic and salt and pepper in a blender or food processor and process until smooth and well mixed.

*3* Remove the chicken from the pan, cover and keep hot. Reduce the heat slightly, then add the pesto to the pan and cook gently, stirring constantly, for a few minutes until the pesto has warmed through.

*4* Pour the warm pesto over the chicken, then garnish with basil leaves and serve with braised baby carrots and celery.

| ——— NUTRITION NOTES ——— | |
| --- | --- |
| Per portion: | |
| Energy | 581kcals/2491kJ |
| Fat, total | 41.9g |
|    saturated fat | 7.67g |
| Protein | 49.12g |
| Carbohydrate | 1.97g |
|    sugar, total | 0.64g |
| Fibre – NSP | 0.6g |
| Sodium | 210mg |

# Thai Chicken and Vegetable Curry

For this curry, chicken and vegetables are cooked in a Thai-spiced coconut sauce.

## Ingredients

### Serves 4

15ml/1 tbsp sunflower oil
6 shallots, finely chopped
2 garlic cloves, crushed
450g/1lb skinless, boneless chicken
    breasts, cut into 1cm/½in cubes
5ml/1 tsp ground coriander
5ml/1 tsp ground cumin
20ml/4 tsp Thai green curry paste
1 green pepper, seeded and diced
175g/6oz baby sweetcorn, halved
115g/4oz French beans, halved
150ml/¼ pint/⅔ cup chicken stock
150ml/¼ pint/⅔ cup coconut milk
30ml/2 tbsp gluten-free cornflour
fresh herb sprigs and toasted cashew
    nuts, to garnish
boiled rice, to serve

*1* Heat the oil in a saucepan, add the shallots, garlic and chicken and cook for 5 minutes until the chicken is coloured all over, stirring occasionally.

*2* Add the coriander, cumin and curry paste and cook for 1 minute.

---
Cook's Tip
---

Add more Thai green curry paste for a hotter curry, if you like.

*3* Add the green pepper, baby sweetcorn, beans, stock and coconut milk and stir to mix.

*4* Bring to the boil, stirring all the time, then cover and simmer for 20–30 minutes until the chicken is tender, stirring occasionally.

*5* Blend the cornflour with about 45ml/3 tbsp water in a small bowl. Stir into the curry, then simmer gently for about 2 minutes, stirring all the time, until the sauce thickens slightly. Serve hot, garnished with fresh herb sprigs and toasted cashew nuts and accompanied by boiled rice.

---
Nutrition Notes
---

Per portion:

| | |
|---|---|
| Energy | 233kcals/9841kJ |
| Fat, total | 6.65g |
| saturated fat | 0.93g |
| Protein | 30.1g |
| Carbohydrate | 14.1g |
| sugar, total | 5g |
| Fibre – NSP | 3.43g |
| Sodium | 924mg |

# Chicken and Leek Pie

Crisp and light gluten-free pastry, flavoured with fresh herbs, tops a tarragon-flavoured chicken and leek sauce to make this tempting savoury pie a popular choice.

## INGREDIENTS

*Serves 4*
175g/6oz/1½ cups gluten-free
  plain flour
pinch of salt
90g/3½oz/7 tbsp sunflower margarine
15ml/1 tbsp chopped fresh mixed herbs
3 leeks, sliced
45ml/3 tbsp gluten-free cornflour
400ml/14fl oz/1⅔ cups semi-
  skimmed milk
15−30ml/1−2 tbsp chopped
  fresh tarragon
350g/12oz cooked, skinless, boneless
  chicken breast, diced
200g/7oz can sweetcorn
  kernels, drained
salt and ground black pepper
fresh herb sprigs and salt flakes,
  to garnish

*1* Make the pastry. Place the flour and salt in a bowl and lightly rub in 75g/3oz/6 tbsp of the margarine until the mixture resembles breadcrumbs. Stir in the mixed herbs and add a little cold water to make smooth, firm dough. Wrap the pastry in a plastic bag and chill for 30 minutes.

*2* Preheat the oven to 190°C/375°F/ Gas 5. Steam the leeks for about 10 minutes until just tender. Drain thoroughly and keep warm.

*3* Meanwhile, blend the cornflour with 75ml/5 tbsp of the milk. Heat the remaining milk in a saucepan until it is just beginning to boil, then pour it on to the cornflour mixture, stirring continuously. Return the mixture to the pan and heat gently until the sauce comes to the boil and thickens, stirring continuously. Simmer gently for about 2 minutes, stirring.

*4* Add the remaining margarine to the pan with the chopped tarragon, leeks, chicken and sweetcorn. Season to taste with salt and pepper and mix together well.

| NUTRITION NOTES | |
| --- | --- |
| Per portion: | |
| Energy | 598kcals/2504kJ |
| Fat, total | 24g |
|   saturated fat | 5.6g |
| Protein | 37.2g |
| Carbohydrate | 59.9g |
|   sugar, total | 9.2g |
| Fibre − NSP | 2.27g |
| Sodium | 265mg |

*5* Spoon the chicken mixture into a 1.2 litre/2 pint/5 cup pie dish and place the dish on a baking sheet. Roll out the pastry to a shape slightly larger than the pie dish. Lay it over the dish, and press to seal. Trim, decorate the top with the trimmings, if liked, and make a slit in the centre.

*6* Bake for 35−40 minutes until the pastry is golden brown. Serve at once, sprinkled with herbs and salt.

| VARIATION |
| --- |
| Use half milk and half chicken or vegetable stock, if preferred. |

# Marinated Monkfish with Tomato Coulis

A light but well-flavoured dish, perfect for summertime eating and enjoying *al fresco* with a glass or two of chilled, fruity wine.

## INGREDIENTS

*Serves 4*

30ml/2 tbsp olive oil
finely grated rind and juice of 1 lime
30ml/2 tbsp chopped fresh mixed herbs
5ml/1 tsp gluten-free Dijon mustard
4 skinless, boneless monkfish fillets
salt and ground black pepper
fresh herb sprigs, to garnish

**For the coulis**

4 plum tomatoes, peeled and chopped
1 garlic clove, chopped
15ml/1 tbsp olive oil
15ml/1 tbsp tomato purée
30ml/2 tbsp chopped fresh oregano
5ml/1 tsp light soft brown sugar

*1* Place the oil, lime rind and juice, herbs, mustard and salt and pepper in a small bowl or jug and whisk together until thoroughly mixed.

--- COOK'S TIP ---

The coulis can be served hot, if you prefer. Simply make as directed in the recipe and heat gently in a saucepan until almost boiling, before serving.

*2* Place the monkfish fillets in a shallow, non-metallic container and pour over the lime mixture. Turn the fish several times in the marinade to coat it. Cover and chill for 1–2 hours.

*3* Meanwhile, make the coulis. Place all the coulis ingredients in a blender or food processor and process until smooth. Season to taste, then cover and chill until required.

*4* Preheat the oven to 180°C/350°F/ Gas 4. Using a fish slice, place each fish fillet on a sheet of greaseproof paper big enough to hold it in a parcel.

*5* Spoon a little marinade over each piece of fish. Gather the paper loosely over the fish and fold over the edges to secure the parcel tightly. Place on a baking sheet.

*6* Bake for 20–30 minutes until the fish fillets are cooked, tender and just beginning to flake.

*7* Carefully unwrap the parcels and serve the fish fillets immediately, with a little of the chilled coulis served alongside, garnished with a few fresh herb sprigs.

--- NUTRITION NOTES ---

Per portion:

| | |
|---|---|
| Energy | 210kcals/821kJ |
| Fat, total | 12.26g |
| saturated fat | 1.82g |
| Protein | 20.75g |
| Carbohydrate | 4.72g |
| sugar, total | 3.8g |
| Fibre – NSP | 1g |
| Sodium | 77mg |

# Baked Trout with Wild Mushrooms

### INGREDIENTS

*Serves 4*
4 whole rainbow trout, cleaned
juice of 1 lemon
15ml/1 tbsp chopped fresh parsley
30ml/2 tbsp olive oil
2 shallots, finely chopped
1 garlic clove, crushed
350g/12oz mixed fresh wild
   mushrooms, chopped
15ml/1 tbsp ruby port or Madeira
30ml/2 tbsp crème fraîche
salt and ground black pepper
chopped fresh parsley, to garnish

*1* Preheat the oven to 180°C/350°F/ Gas 4. Place the trout, side by side, in a lightly greased, shallow, ovenproof dish. Pour over the lemon juice and sprinkle over the parsley.

*2* Cover with foil and bake for 30–40 minutes until the fish is cooked, tender and beginning to flake.

*3* Meanwhile, heat the oil in a frying pan, add the shallots and garlic and cook gently for 3–5 minutes until the shallots have softened, stirring them occasionally. Add the mushrooms and cook gently for about 5 minutes until they are just cooked, stirring frequently.

*4* Add the port or Madeira, increase the heat and cook, stirring, for a few minutes until most of the liquid has evaporated. Add the crème fraîche, season to taste with salt and pepper and mix well.

*5* Place the cooked trout on four warmed serving plates and spoon a little of the mushroom sauce over each fish or on either side of it. Sprinkle a little chopped parsley over each fish and serve immediately.

| NUTRITION NOTES | |
| --- | --- |
| Per portion: | |
| Energy | 330kcals/924kJ |
| Fat, total | 18.4g |
| saturated fat | 3.9g |
| Protein | 38.3g |
| Carbohydrate | 1.92g |
| sugar, total | 1.62g |
| Fibre – NSP | 1.3g |
| Sodium | 102mg |

# Chargrilled Salmon Steaks with Mango Salsa

### INGREDIENTS

*Serves 4*
1 medium, ripe mango
115g/4oz cucumber
2 spring onions
30ml/2 tbsp chopped fresh coriander
4 salmon steaks, each about 175g/6oz
juice of 1 lemon or lime
salt and ground black pepper
fresh coriander sprigs and lemon
   wedges, to garnish

*1* Make the mango salsa. Peel and stone the mango, finely chop the flesh and place in a bowl. Peel, seed and finely chop the cucumber; chop the spring onions. Add to the mango with the coriander and salt and pepper. Mix, cover and leave for 30 minutes.

*2* While the salsa is standing to allow the flavours to mingle, preheat a barbecue or grill. Place the salmon steaks on a ridged grill pan, drizzle over the lemon or lime juice and cook for about 6 minutes on each side until the steaks are tender and just beginning to flake. Alternatively, cook over a hot barbecue or under a moderate grill.

*3* Transfer the salmon to serving plates, spoon some mango salsa alongside each steak and serve immediately, garnished with coriander sprigs and lemon wedges.

| NUTRITION NOTES | |
| --- | --- |
| Per portion: | |
| Energy | 350kcals/1460kJ |
| Fat, total | 19.5g |
| saturated fat | 3.4g |
| Protein | 36.2g |
| Carbohydrate | 7.84g |
| sugar, total | 4.3g |
| Fibre – NSP | 2g |
| Sodium | 98mg |

# Tuna, Courgette and Pepper Frittata

This nutritious Italian omelette is quick and easy to make. Serve it simply, with a lightly dressed mixed or green leaf salad.

### INGREDIENTS

*Serves 4*
15ml/1 tbsp sunflower oil
1 onion, chopped
1 courgette, thinly sliced
1 red pepper, seeded and sliced
4 eggs
30ml/2 tbsp semi-skimmed milk
200g/7oz can tuna in brine or water, drained and flaked
10ml/2 tsp dried herbes de Provence
50g/2oz/½ cup grated Red Leicester cheese
salt and ground black pepper
mixed or green leaf salad, to serve

*1* Heat half the oil in a shallow saucepan, add the onion, courgette and red pepper and cook for 5 minutes, stirring frequently.

*2* Beat the eggs with the milk in a small bowl. Heat the remaining oil in a heavy-based omelette pan. Add the cooked courgette and red pepper, flaked tuna and herbs, and season well.

*3* Pour the egg mixture into the frying pan on top of the vegetable mixture and cook over a medium heat until the eggs are beginning to set. Pull the sides into the middle to allow the uncooked egg to run on to the pan, then continue cooking undisturbed until the frittata is golden underneath. Meanwhile, preheat the grill.

*4* Sprinkle the cheese over the top of the frittata and grill until the cheese has melted and the top is golden.

*5* Cut the frittata into wedges and serve immediately with a mixed or green leaf salad.

| NUTRITION NOTES | |
|---|---|
| Per portion: | |
| Energy | 250kcals/1046kJ |
| Fat, total | 15.3g |
| saturated fat | 5.2g |
| Protein | 24g |
| Carbohydrate | 4.7g |
| sugar, total | 3.1g |
| Fibre – NSP | 0.8g |
| Sodium | 330mg |

# Cod, Tomato and Pepper Bake

The wonderful sun-drenched flavours of the Mediterranean are brought together in this appetizing, potato-topped bake. Lightly cooked courgettes make a tasty accompaniment.

### INGREDIENTS

*Serves 4*
450g/1lb potatoes, cut into
  thin slices
30ml/2 tbsp olive oil
1 red onion, chopped
1 garlic clove, crushed
1 red pepper, seeded and diced
1 yellow pepper, seeded and diced
225g/8oz mushrooms, sliced
400g/14oz and 225g/8oz cans
  chopped tomatoes
150ml/¼ pint/⅔ cup dry white wine
450g/1lb skinless, boneless cod fillet,
  cut into 2 cm/¾in cubes
50g/2oz/½ cup pitted black
  olives, chopped
15ml/1 tbsp chopped fresh basil
15ml/1 tbsp chopped fresh oregano
salt and ground black pepper
fresh oregano sprigs, to garnish
cooked courgettes, to serve

*1* Preheat the oven to 200°C/400°F/ Gas 6. Par-boil the potatoes in a saucepan of lightly salted, boiling water for 4 minutes. Drain thoroughly, then add 15ml/1 tbsp of the oil and toss together to mix. Set aside.

*2* Heat the remaining oil in a saucepan, add the onion, garlic and red and yellow peppers and cook for 5 minutes, stirring occasionally.

*3* Stir in the mushrooms, tomatoes and wine, bring to the boil and boil rapidly for a few minutes until the sauce has reduced slightly.

——— NUTRITION NOTES ———

Per portion:

| | |
|---|---:|
| Energy | 336kcals/1412kJ |
| Fat, total | 10.6g |
| saturated fat | 1.5g |
| Protein | 26.5g |
| Carbohydrate | 29.2g |
| sugar, total | 9g |
| Fibre – NSP | 4.6g |
| Sodium | 424mg |

*4* Add the fish, olives, herbs and seasoning to the tomato mixture.

*5* Spoon the mixture into a lightly greased casserole and arrange the potato slices over the top, covering the fish mixture completely.

*6* Bake, uncovered, for about 45 minutes until the fish is cooked and tender and the potato topping is browned. Garnish with fresh oregano sprigs and serve with courgettes.

# VEGETARIAN DISHES

*If you prefer to follow a vegetarian diet or to choose a vegetarian dish as an alternative to meat, this chapter has a collection of appetizing and nutritious, gluten-free recipes, such as Vegetable Moussaka, Provençal Stuffed Peppers, Herby Rice Pilaf and Wild Mushroom and Broccoli Flan. Serve the dishes with fresh gluten-free bread or pasta, potatoes or rice and a mixed leaf salad or cooked vegetables.*

# Vegetable Moussaka

This is a really flavoursome vegetarian alternative to classic meat moussaka. Serve it with warm, gluten-free bread and a glass or two of rustic red wine.

## INGREDIENTS

*Serves 6*
450g/1lb aubergines, sliced
115g/4oz whole green lentils
600ml/1 pint/2½ cups vegetable stock
1 bay leaf
45ml/3 tbsp olive oil
1 onion, sliced
1 garlic clove, crushed
225g/8oz mushrooms, sliced
400g/14oz can chick-peas, rinsed
  and drained
400g/14oz can chopped tomatoes
30ml/2 tbsp tomato purée
10ml/2 tsp dried herbes de Provence
45ml/3 tbsp water
300ml/½ pint/1¼ cups natural yogurt
3 eggs
50g/2oz/½ cup grated mature
  Cheddar cheese
salt and ground black pepper
flat leaf parsley sprigs, to garnish

*1* Sprinkle the aubergine slices with salt and place in a colander. Cover and leave for 30 minutes to allow the bitter juices to be extracted.

*2* Meanwhile, place the lentils, stock and bay leaf in a saucepan. Cover, bring to the boil and simmer for about 20 minutes until the lentils are just tender. Drain well and keep warm.

*3* Heat 15ml/1 tbsp of the oil in a large saucepan, add the onion and garlic and cook for 5 minutes, stirring. Stir in the lentils, mushrooms, chick-peas, tomatoes, tomato purée, herbs and water. Bring to the boil, cover and simmer gently for 10 minutes.

*4* Preheat the oven to 180°C/350°F/Gas 4. Rinse the aubergine slices, drain and pat dry. Heat the remaining oil in a frying pan and fry the slices in batches for 3–4 minutes, turning once.

*5* Season the lentil mixture with salt and pepper. Arrange a layer of aubergine slices in the bottom of a large, shallow, ovenproof dish or roasting tin, then spoon over a layer of the lentil mixture. Continue the layers until all the aubergines slices and lentil mixture are used up.

*6* Beat together the yogurt, eggs and salt and pepper and pour the mixture into the dish. Sprinkle the grated cheese on top and bake for about 45 minutes until the topping is golden brown and bubbling. Serve immediately, garnished with flat leaf parsley sprigs.

| NUTRITION NOTES | |
|---|---|
| Per portion: | |
| Energy | 348kcals/1463kJ |
| Fat, total | 17.3g |
| saturated fat | 4.4g |
| Protein | 20.6g |
| Carbohydrate | 29.5g |
| sugar, total | 9g |
| Fibre – NSP | 7.1g |
| Sodium | 722mg |

# Rice Noodles with Vegetable Chilli Sauce

## INGREDIENTS

### Serves 4

15ml/1 tbsp sunflower oil
1 onion, chopped
2 garlic cloves, crushed
1 fresh red chilli, seeded and
   finely chopped
1 red pepper, seeded and diced
2 carrots, finely chopped
175g/6oz baby sweetcorn, halved
225g/8oz can sliced bamboo shoots,
   rinsed and drained
400g/14oz can red kidney beans, rinsed
   and drained
300ml/½ pint/1¼ cups passata or
   sieved tomatoes
15ml/1 tbsp gluten-free soy sauce
5ml/1 tsp ground coriander
250g/9oz rice noodles
30ml/2 tbsp chopped fresh coriander
   or parsley
salt and ground black pepper
fresh parsley sprigs, to garnish

*1* Heat the oil, add the onion, garlic, chilli and red pepper and cook for 5 minutes, stirring. Stir in the carrots, sweetcorn, bamboo shoots, kidney beans, passata or sieved tomatoes, soy sauce and ground coriander.

--- COOK'S TIP ---

After handling chillies, wash your hands. Chillies contain volatile oils that can irritate and burn sensitive areas, such as the eyes, if they are touched.

*2* Bring to the boil, then cover, reduce the heat, and simmer gently for 30 minutes until the vegetables are tender, stirring occasionally. Season with salt and pepper to taste.

*3* Meanwhile, place the noodles in a bowl and cover with boiling water. Stir with a fork and leave to stand for 3–4 minutes, or according to the packet instructions. Rinse with boiling water and drain thoroughly.

*4* Stir the coriander or parsley into the sauce. Spoon the noodles on to warmed serving plates and top with the sauce. Garnish with parsley and serve.

--- NUTRITION NOTES ---

Per portion:

| | |
|---|---|
| Energy | 409kcals/1717kJ |
| Fat, total | 5.2g |
| saturated fat | 0.6g |
| Protein | 13.5g |
| Carbohydrate | 77.3g |
| sugar, total | 10.6g |
| Fibre – NSP | 8.7g |
| Sodium | 1156mg |

# Harvest Vegetable and Lentil Casserole

## INGREDIENTS

*Serves 6*

15ml/1 tbsp sunflower oil
2 leeks, sliced
1 garlic clove, crushed
4 celery sticks, chopped
2 carrots, sliced
2 parsnips, diced
1 sweet potato, diced
225g/8oz swede, diced
175g/6oz whole brown
  or green lentils
450g/1lb tomatoes, skinned, seeded
  and chopped
15ml/1 tbsp chopped fresh thyme
15ml/1 tbsp chopped fresh marjoram
900ml/1½ pints/3¾ cups well-
  flavoured vegetable stock
15ml/1 tbsp gluten-free cornflour
salt and ground black pepper
fresh thyme sprigs, to garnish

*1* Preheat the oven to 180°C/350°F/
Gas 4. Heat the oil in a large
flameproof casserole. Add the leeks,
garlic and celery and cook over a low
heat for 3 minutes, stirring occasionally.

—— NUTRITION NOTES ——

Per portion:

| | |
|---|---|
| Energy | 254kcals/1075kJ |
| Fat, total | 11g |
|   saturated fat | 0.15g |
| Protein | 11.5g |
| Carbohydrate | 37.8g |
|   sugar, total | 10.8g |
| Fibre – NSP | 7.1g |
| Sodium | 722mg |

*2* Add the carrots, parsnips, sweet
potato, swede, lentils, tomatoes,
herbs, stock and seasoning. Stir well.
Bring to the boil, stirring occasionally.

*3* Cover and bake for about
50 minutes until the vegetables and
lentils are cooked and tender, removing
the casserole from the oven and stirring
the vegetable mixture once or twice
during the cooking time.

*4* Remove the casserole from the
oven. Blend the cornflour with
45ml/3 tbsp water in a small bowl. Stir
it into the casserole and heat gently,
stirring continuously, until the mixture
comes to the boil and thickens, then
simmer gently for 2 minutes, stirring.

*5* Spoon the casserole on to warmed
serving plates or into bowls and
serve garnished with thyme sprigs.

# Herby Rice Pilaf

A quick and easy recipe to make, this simple pilaf is delicious to eat. Serve with a selection of cooked fresh seasonal vegetables such as broccoli florets, baby sweetcorn and carrots.

### INGREDIENTS

*Serves 4*
225g/8oz mixed brown basmati and
   wild rice
15ml/1 tbsp olive oil
1 onion, chopped
1 garlic clove, crushed
5ml/1 tsp each ground cumin and
   ground turmeric
50g/2oz/½ cup sultanas
750ml/1¼ pints/3 cups vegetable stock
30–45ml/2–3 tbsp chopped fresh
   mixed herbs
salt and ground black pepper
fresh herb sprigs and 25g/1oz/¼ cup
   pistachio nuts, chopped, to garnish

*1* Wash the rice in a sieve under cold running water, then drain well. Heat the oil in a saucepan, add the onion and garlic and cook gently for 5 minutes, stirring occasionally.

*2* Add the spices and rice and cook gently for 1 minute, stirring. Stir in the sultanas and stock, then bring to the boil, cover and simmer gently for 20–25 minutes until the rice is cooked and just tender and almost all the liquid has been absorbed, stirring occasionally.

*3* Stir in the chopped mixed herbs and season to taste with salt and pepper. Spoon the pilaf into a warmed serving dish and garnish with fresh herb sprigs and a scattering of chopped pistachio nuts. Serve immediately.

| ——— NUTRITION NOTES ——— | |
| --- | --- |
| Per portion: | |
| Energy | 326kcals/1363kJ |
| Fat, total | 8.6g |
|   saturated fat | 0.15g |
| Protein | 1.0g |
| Carbohydrate | 56g |
|   sugar, total | 10.2g |
| Fibre – NSP | 1.4g |
| Sodium | 630mg |

# Cheese-topped Roast Baby Vegetables

A simple way of serving baby vegetables that really brings out their flavour.

### INGREDIENTS

*Serves 6*
1kg/2¼lb mixed baby vegetables, such
   as aubergines, onions or shallots,
   courgettes, sweetcorn and button
   mushrooms
1 red pepper, seeded and cut into
   large pieces
1–2 garlic cloves, finely chopped
15–30ml/1–2 tbsp olive oil
30ml/2 tbsp chopped fresh mixed herbs
225g/8oz cherry tomatoes
115g/4oz/1 cup coarsely grated
   mozzarella cheese
salt and ground black pepper
black olives, to serve (optional)

*1* Preheat the oven to 220°C/425°F/ Gas 7. Cut all the mixed baby vegetables in half lengthways.

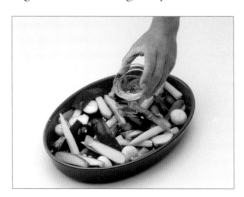

*2* Place the baby vegetables and peppers in an ovenproof dish with the garlic and seasoning. Drizzle the oil over and toss the vegetables to coat them. Bake for 20 minutes until tinged brown at the edges, stirring once.

*3* Remove the dish from the oven and stir in the herbs. Scatter the tomatoes over the surface and top with the mozzarella cheese. Return to the oven and bake for 5–10 minutes more until the cheese has melted and is bubbling. Serve at once, with black olives, if liked.

| ——— NUTRITION NOTES ——— | |
| --- | --- |
| Per portion: | |
| Energy | 162kcals/679kJ |
| Fat, total | 10g |
|   saturated fat | 3.4g |
| Protein | 8.2g |
| Carbohydrate | 10.6g |
|   sugar, total | 7g |
| Fibre – NSP | 3.1g |
| Sodium | 172mg |

# Wild Mushroom and Broccoli Flan

Gluten-free potato and cheese pastry combines well with a mushroom and broccoli filling to ensure this savoury flan is a family favourite. Lightly cooked, sliced leeks can be used instead of broccoli florets, if preferred.

## INGREDIENTS

### Serves 8
115g/4oz small broccoli florets
15ml/1 tbsp olive oil
3 shallots, finely chopped
175g/6oz mixed wild mushrooms, such as ceps, shiitake mushrooms and oyster mushrooms, sliced or chopped
2 eggs
200ml/7fl oz/scant 1 cup semi-skimmed milk
15ml/1 tbsp chopped fresh tarragon
50g/2oz/½ cup grated Cheddar cheese
salt and ground black pepper
fresh herb sprigs, to garnish

### For the pastry
75g/3oz/¾ cup brown rice flour
75g/3oz/¾ cup gluten-free cornmeal
pinch of salt
75g/3oz/6 tbsp soft margarine
115g/4oz cold mashed potatoes
50g/2oz/½ cup grated Cheddar cheese

*1* First make the pastry. Place the rice flour, cornmeal and salt in a mixing bowl and stir to mix. Lightly rub in the margarine with your fingertips until the mixture resembles breadcrumbs.

*2* Stir in the mashed potatoes and cheese and mix to form a smooth, soft dough. Wrap in a plastic bag and chill for 30 minutes.

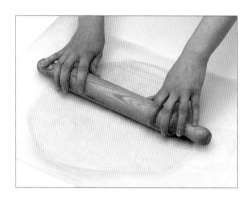

*3* Roll out the pastry between two sheets of greaseproof paper and use to line a 24cm/9½in loose-bottomed flan tin, gently pressing the pastry into the sides of the flan tin. Carefully trim around the top edge of the pastry case with a sharp knife. Chill the pastry while making the filling.

*4* Preheat the oven to 200°C/400°F/Gas 6. Cook the broccoli florets in a saucepan of lightly salted, boiling water for 3 minutes. Drain thoroughly and set aside.

*5* Heat the oil in a frying pan, add the shallots and cook gently for 3 minutes, stirring. Add the mushrooms and cook gently for 2 minutes.

*6* Spoon into the pastry case and top with broccoli. Beat the eggs, milk, tarragon and seasoning together and pour over the vegetables. Top with cheese. Bake for 10 minutes, reduce the oven temperature to 180°C/350°F/Gas 4 and bake for about 30 minutes until lightly set. Serve warm or cold, garnished with fresh herbs.

*Right: Savoury Nut Loaf (top) and Wild Mushroom and Broccoli Flan.*

| ——— NUTRITION NOTES ——— | |
| --- | --- |
| Per portion: | |
| Energy | 265kcals/1102kJ |
| Fat, total | 17.2g |
| saturated fat | 5.54g |
| Protein | 8.8g |
| Carbohydrate | 18.5g |
| sugar, total | 1.95g |
| Fibre – NSP | 1g |
| Sodium | 209mg |

# Savoury Nut Loaf

This delicious nut loaf makes perfect picnic food.

## INGREDIENTS

*Serves 8*

15ml/1 tbsp olive oil
1 onion, chopped
1 leek, chopped
2 celery sticks, finely chopped
225g/8oz mushrooms, chopped
2 garlic cloves, crushed
425g/15oz can lentils, rinsed
  and drained
115g/4oz/1 cup mixed nuts, such as
  hazelnuts, cashew nuts and almonds,
  finely chopped
50g/2oz potato flour
50g/2oz/½ cup grated mature
  Cheddar cheese
1 egg, beaten
45–60ml/3–4 tbsp chopped fresh
  mixed herbs
salt and ground black pepper
flat leaf parsley sprigs, to garnish

*1* Preheat the oven to 190°C/375°F/ Gas 5. Lightly grease and line the base and sides of a 900g/2lb loaf tin.

*2* Heat the oil in a large saucepan, add the chopped onion, leek, celery and mushrooms and the crushed garlic, then cook gently for 10 minutes until the vegetables have softened, stirring occasionally.

*3* Add the lentils, mixed nuts, potato flour, grated cheese, egg and herbs to the pan. Season with salt and pepper and mix thoroughly.

*4* Spoon the nut, vegetable and lentil mixture into the prepared loaf tin and level the surface. Bake, uncovered, for 50–60 minutes or until the nut loaf is lightly browned on top and firm to the touch.

*5* Cool the loaf slightly in the tin, then turn it out on to a large serving plate. Serve hot or cold, cut into slices, and garnished with flat leaf parsley sprigs.

| NUTRITION NOTES | |
| --- | --- |
| Per portion: | |
| Energy | 230kcals/953kJ |
| Fat, total | 13.1g |
| saturated fat | 2.9g |
| Protein | 12.5g |
| Carbohydrate | 16.8g |
| sugar, total | 1.9g |
| Fibre – NSP | 4.3g |
| Sodium | 67mg |

# Provençal Stuffed Peppers

## INGREDIENTS

*Serves 4*

15ml/1 tbsp olive oil
1 red onion, sliced
1 courgette, diced
115g/4oz mushrooms, sliced
1 garlic clove, crushed
400g/14oz can chopped tomatoes
15ml/1 tbsp tomato purée
40g/1½oz/scant ⅓ cup pine nuts
30ml/2 tbsp chopped fresh basil
4 large peppers
50g/2oz/½ cup finely grated Red
   Leicester cheese
salt and ground black pepper
fresh basil leaves, to garnish

*1* Preheat the oven to 180°C/350°F/ Gas 4. Heat the oil in a pan, add the onion, courgette, mushrooms and garlic and cook gently for 3 minutes, stirring occasionally.

*2* Stir in the tomatoes and tomato purée, then bring to the boil and simmer, uncovered, for 10–15 minutes, stirring occasionally, until thickened slightly. Remove from the heat and stir in the pine nuts, basil and seasoning.

*3* Cut the peppers in half lengthways and seed them. Blanch in a pan of boiling water for 3 minutes. Drain.

*4* Place in a shallow, ovenproof dish and fill with the vegetable mixture.

*5* Cover the dish with foil and bake for 20 minutes. Remove the foil, sprinkle each pepper with a little grated cheese and bake, uncovered, for a further 5–10 minutes until the cheese is melted and bubbling. Garnish with basil leaves and serve at once.

---
#### VARIATIONS

Use the vegetable sauce to stuff other vegetables, such as large courgettes or baby aubergines, in place of the peppers. Try grated Parmesan in place of Red Leicester.

---
#### NUTRITION NOTES

| Per portion: | |
| --- | --- |
| Energy | 211kcals/881kJ |
| Fat, total | 15.7g |
| saturated fat | 3.8g |
| Protein | 8.2g |
| Carbohydrate | 10g |
| sugar, total | 8.6g |
| Fibre – NSP | 4.1g |
| Sodium | 136mg |

# Mixed Mushroom and Parmesan Risotto

A classic risotto of mixed mushrooms, herbs and fresh Parmesan cheese, best simply served with a mixed leaf salad tossed in a light dressing.

### INGREDIENTS

*Serves 4*
15ml/1 tbsp olive oil
4 shallots, finely chopped
2 garlic cloves, crushed
10g/¼oz dried porcini mushrooms, soaked in 150ml/¼ pint/⅔ cup hot water for 20 minutes
450g/1lb mixed mushrooms, such as closed cup, chestnut and field mushrooms, sliced or chopped
250g/9oz long grain brown rice
900ml/1½ pints/3¾ cups well-flavoured vegetable stock
30–45ml/2–3 tbsp chopped fresh flat leaf parsley
50g/2oz/⅔ cup grated Parmesan cheese
salt and ground black pepper

*1* Heat the oil in a large saucepan, add the shallots and garlic and cook gently for 5 minutes, stirring. Drain the porcini, reserving their liquid, and chop roughly. Add all the mushrooms to the pan along with the porcini soaking liquid, the brown rice and 300ml/½ pint/1¼ cups of the stock.

*2* Bring to the boil, reduce the heat and simmer, uncovered, until all the liquid has been absorbed, stirring frequently. Add a ladleful of hot stock and stir until it has been absorbed.

*3* Continue cooking and adding the hot stock, a ladleful at a time, until the rice is cooked and creamy but *al dente*, stirring frequently. This should take about 35 minutes and it may not be necessary to add all the stock.

*4* Season with salt and pepper to taste, stir in the chopped parsley and grated Parmesan and serve at once. Alternatively, sprinkle the Parmesan over the risotto just before serving.

| NUTRITION NOTES | |
| --- | --- |
| Per portion: | |
| Energy | 358kcals/1511kJ |
| Fat, total | 10.9g |
| saturated fat | 3.65g |
| Protein | 12.8g |
| Carbohydrate | 55.4g |
| sugar, total | 2.2g |
| Fibre – NSP | 3.4g |
| Sodium | 738mg |

# Spring Vegetable Omelette

### INGREDIENTS

*Serves 4*
50g/2oz asparagus tips
50g/2oz spring greens, shredded
15ml/1 tbsp sunflower oil
1 onion, sliced
175g/6oz cooked baby new potatoes, halved or diced
2 tomatoes, chopped
6 eggs
15–30ml/1–2 tbsp chopped fresh mixed herbs
salt and ground black pepper
salad, to serve

*1* Steam the asparagus tips and spring greens over a saucepan of boiling water for 5–10 minutes until tender. Drain the vegetables and keep warm.

*2* Heat the oil in a large frying pan, add the onion and cook gently for 5–10 minutes until softened, stirring.

*3* Add the baby potatoes and cook for 3 minutes, stirring. Stir in the tomatoes, asparagus and spring greens. Lightly beat the eggs with the herbs and season with salt and pepper.

*4* Pour the eggs over the vegetables, then cook over a gentle heat until the bottom of the omelette is golden brown. Preheat the grill to hot and cook the omelette under the grill for 2–3 minutes until the top is golden brown. Serve with salad.

| NUTRITION NOTES | |
| --- | --- |
| Per portion: | |
| Energy | 221kcals/923kJ |
| Fat, total | 14.2g |
| saturated fat | 3.4g |
| Protein | 13.6g |
| Carbohydrate | 10.4g |
| sugar, total | 3.4g |
| Fibre – NSP | 2.1g |
| Sodium | 142mg |

# DESSERTS

*Desserts are often the most tempting part of a meal, but they don't have to be naughty to be nice! These delicious and healthy, gluten-free desserts include special occasion treats, such as Summer Strawberry Roulade and a rich chocolate mousse served with glazed kumquats, and scrumptious family fare, such as Creamy Lemon Rice and Mango Yogurt Ice. Plain or Greek yogurt, fromage frais, gluten-free custard, dairy cream or crème fraîche make excellent accompaniments.*

# Creamy Lemon Rice

This is a creamy baked rice pudding with a difference, being subtly flavoured with lemon. It is wonderful served warm or cold with fresh strawberries.

### INGREDIENTS

*Serves 4*

50g/2oz/ ¼ cup short grain white rice
600ml/1 pint/2½ cups semi-
  skimmed milk
25g/1oz/2 tbsp caster sugar
finely grated rind of 1 lemon
15g/ ½oz/1 tbsp butter, cut into
  small pieces
pared orange and lemon rind,
  to decorate

### For serving

225g/8oz prepared fresh fruit, such
  as strawberries or pineapple
90ml/6 tbsp reduced-fat crème
  fraîche (optional)

*1* Lightly grease a 900ml/1½ pint/
3¾ cup ovenproof dish. Add the rice and pour in the milk, then set aside for about 30 minutes, to allow the rice to soften a little. Preheat the oven to 150°C/300°F/Gas 2.

*2* Add the caster sugar, grated lemon rind and butter to the rice and milk and stir gently to mix. Bake for 2–2½ hours until the top of the pudding is lightly browned.

*3* Decorate with pared orange and lemon rind and serve warm or cold with the fresh fruit.

*4* If serving cold, allow the pudding to cool, remove and discard the skin, then chill. Fold in the crème fraîche just before serving, if liked.

| NUTRITION NOTES | |
|---|---|
| Per portion: | |
| Energy | 220kcals/928kJ |
| Fat, total | 8.8g |
|   saturated fat | 3.9g |
| Protein | 6.8g |
| Carbohydrate | 30.4g |
|   sugar, total | 19.7g |
| Fibre – NSP | 0.7g |
| Sodium | 121mg |

---

# Peach and Raspberry Crumble

### INGREDIENTS

*Serves 4*

75g/3oz/ ¾ cup brown rice flour
50g/2oz/4 tbsp soft margarine
25g/1oz/ ¼ cup buckwheat flakes
25g/1oz/ ¼ cup millet flakes
25g/1oz/ ¼ cup hazelnuts,
  roughly chopped
75g/3oz/scant ⅓ cup soft light
  brown sugar
5ml/1 tsp ground ginger
3 fresh peaches, stoned and cut
  into wedges
225g/8oz/1⅓ cups raspberries
60ml/4 tbsp fresh orange juice

*1* Preheat the oven to 180°C/350°F/
Gas 4. Grease a 1.2 litre/2 pint/
5 cup pie dish. Place the rice flour in a bowl and rub in the margarine until the mixture resembles breadcrumbs.

*2* Stir in the buckwheat flakes, millet flakes, hazelnuts, 50g/2oz/ ¼ cup of the sugar and the ginger. Mix well.

*3* Mix the peaches, raspberries, orange juice and remaining sugar together and place in the dish. Sprinkle the crumble over the top, pressing it down lightly. Bake for 30–45 minutes, until the crumble is lightly browned. Serve warm or cold.

| VARIATIONS | |
|---|---|

Use almonds or walnuts, in place of the hazelnuts and substitute ground cinnamon for the ground ginger.

  Firm, ripe nectarines or thinly sliced dessert apples could be used in place of the peaches, if you like.

| NUTRITION NOTES | |
|---|---|
| Per portion: | |
| Energy | 369kcals/1546kJ |
| Fat, total | 14.4g |
|   saturated fat | 2.5g |
| Protein | 4.8g |
| Carbohydrate | 57.5g |
|   sugar, total | 31.8g |
| Fibre – NSP | 3.1g |
| Sodium | 108mg |

# Summer Strawberry Roulade

### INGREDIENTS

*Serves 8*

3 eggs
115g/4oz/ ½ cup caster sugar, plus
    30ml/2 tbsp extra for sprinkling
115g/4oz/1 cup gluten-free plain flour
150g/5oz/⅔ cup Greek yogurt
150g/5oz/⅔ cup plain fromage frais
225g/8oz/2 cups strawberries, sliced
strawberries and sprigs of mint,
    to decorate

*1* Preheat the oven to 200°C/400°F/ Gas 6. Place the eggs and the 115g/4oz/ ½ cup caster sugar in a large bowl over a pan of simmering water. Whisk, using an electric hand whisk, until the mixture is pale, creamy and thick enough to leave a trail on the surface when the whisk is lifted.

*2* Remove the bowl from the heat and whisk the mixture until cool. Sift half the flour over it, then fold in gently using a metal spoon. Sift the remaining flour over and fold in with 15ml/1 tbsp hot water.

*3* Pour it into a greased and lined 33 x 23cm/13 x 9in Swiss roll tin, tilting the tin to level the surface.

*4* Bake for 10–15 minutes or until well-risen, golden brown and firm to the touch. Meanwhile, sprinkle a sheet of non-stick baking paper with the remaining caster sugar. Turn out the hot cake on to the paper, trim off the crusty edges and quickly roll up the cake with the paper inside. Place seam-side down on a wire rack and allow to cool completely.

*5* Once it has cooled, carefully unroll the cake. Mix together the Greek yogurt and fromage frais and spread evenly over the cake. Scatter the sliced strawberries over the top. Carefully reroll the cake and serve immediately, in slices, garnished with strawberries and sprigs of mint.

| NUTRITION NOTES | |
|---|---|
| Per portion: | |
| Energy | 190kcals/797kJ |
| Fat, total | 5.68g |
| saturated fat | 2.5g |
| Protein | 6.5g |
| Carbohydrate | 29.3g |
| sugar, total | 18.8g |
| Fibre – NSP | 0.3g |
| Sodium | 53mg |

# Apple and Cinnamon Buckwheat Pancakes

Spiced pan-fried apple slices create a scrumptious topping for these buckwheat pancakes.

## INGREDIENTS

*Serves 4*

3 cooking apples, peeled, cored
   and sliced
50g/2oz/¼ cup caster sugar
50g/2oz/4 tbsp unsalted butter
30–45ml/2–3 tbsp brandy
5–10ml/1–2 tsp ground cinnamon
fresh mint sprigs, to garnish
crème fraîche, to serve

**For the pancakes**
50g/2oz/½ cup buckwheat flour
50g/2oz/½ cup rice flour
pinch of salt
1 egg
300ml/½ pint/1½ cups semi-
   skimmed milk
sunflower oil, for frying

*1* Make the pancakes. Place the buckwheat flour, rice flour and salt in a bowl and make a well in the centre of the flour. Break in the egg and add a little of the milk, beating well with a wooden spoon.

*2* Gradually beat in the remaining milk, drawing the flour in from the sides to make a smooth batter.

*3* Heat a little oil in an 18cm/7in non-stick frying pan. Pour in enough batter to coat the base of the pan thinly. Cook until golden brown, then turn and cook on the other side.

*4* Transfer the cooked pancake to a warmed plate and keep hot. Repeat with the remaining batter to make eight pancakes in all. Place the cooked pancakes on top of one another with greaseproof paper in between to prevent them sticking together.

*5* Toss the apple slices in the caster sugar in a mixing bowl.

*6* Melt the butter in a large frying pan, add the apple slices to the pan and cook over a high heat for about 5 minutes until the apple slices soften slightly and the sugar has caramelized, stirring frequently. Remove the pan from the heat and sprinkle the apples with the brandy and cinnamon.

*7* Serve the pancakes topped with the cooked apples and accompanied by some crème fraîche sprinkled with a little extra ground cinnamon, if liked, and garnished with mint.

| NUTRITION NOTES | |
|---|---|
| Per portion: | |
| Energy | 368kcals/1541kJ |
| Fat, total | 16.1g |
| saturated fat | 3.6g |
| Protein | 6.5g |
| Carbohydrate | 47.8g |
| sugar, total | 27.3g |
| Fibre – NSP | 1.7g |
| Sodium | 151mg |

# Chocolate Meringues with Mixed Fruit Compote

Mini chocolate meringues are sandwiched with crème fraîche and served with a compote of mixed summer berries to make this impressive dessert.

## INGREDIENTS

*Serves 6*

105ml/7 tbsp unsweetened red grape juice
105ml/7 tbsp unsweetened apple juice
30ml/2 tbsp clear honey
450g/1lb mixed fresh berries, such as blackcurrants, redcurrants, raspberries and blackberries

**For the meringues**
3 egg whites
175g/6oz/¾ cup caster sugar
75g/3oz good-quality plain chocolate, finely grated
175g/6oz/¾ cup reduced-fat crème fraîche

---

NUTRITION NOTES

Per portion:
| | |
|---|---|
| Energy | 292kcals/1235kJ |
| Fat, total | 9.48g |
| saturated fat | 5.7g |
| Protein | 3.8g |
| Carbohydrate | 51.2g |
| sugar, total | 51.1g |
| Fibre – NSP | 1.7g |
| Sodium | 49.8mg |

*1* Preheat the oven to 110°C/225°F/ Gas ¼. Grease and line two baking sheets with non-stick baking paper.

*2* Make the meringues. Whisk the egg whites in a large bowl until stiff. Gradually whisk in half the caster sugar, then fold in the remaining sugar, using a metal spoon. Gently fold in the grated chocolate.

*3* Spoon the meringue mixture into a large piping bag fitted with a large star nozzle. Pipe small rounds on to the prepared baking sheets.

*4* Bake for 2½–3 hours until the meringues are firm and crisp, then transfer to a wire rack to cool.

*5* Meanwhile, make the compote. Heat the fruit juices in a saucepan with the honey until almost boiling.

*6* Place the mixed fresh berries in a large bowl and pour over the hot fruit juice and honey mixture. Stir gently to mix, then set aside and leave to cool. Once cool, cover the bowl and chill until required.

*7* When ready to serve, sandwich the cold meringues with the crème fraîche and arrange them on a serving plate or dish.

*8* Serve the meringues immediately on individual plates with the mixed fruit compote.

# Rich Chocolate Mousse with Glazed Kumquats

## INGREDIENTS

*Serves 6*
225g/8oz plain chocolate, broken
   into squares
4 eggs, separated
30ml/2 tbsp brandy or orange liqueur
90ml/6 tbsp double cream

**For the glazed kumquats**
275g/10oz kumquats
115g/4oz/ ½ cup granulated sugar
15ml/1 tbsp orange liqueur

*1* Make the glazed kumquats. Slice the fruit and place cut face up in a shallow serving dish.

*2* Place the sugar in a saucepan with 150ml/ ¼ pint/ ⅔ cup water. Heat gently, stirring constantly, until the sugar has dissolved, then bring to the boil and boil rapidly, without stirring, until a golden-brown caramel forms.

*3* Remove the pan from the heat and very carefully stir in 60ml/4 tbsp boiling water to dissolve the caramel. Stir in the orange liqueur, then pour the caramel over the kumquat slices and leave to cool. Once completely cold, cover and chill.

*4* Make the chocolate mousse. Line a shallow 20cm/8in round cake tin with clear film. Melt the chocolate in a bowl over a pan of simmering water, then remove the bowl from the heat.

*5* Beat the egg yolks and brandy or liqueur into the chocolate, then fold in the cream, mixing well. In a separate clean bowl, whisk the egg whites until stiff, then gently fold them into the chocolate mixture.

*6* Pour the mixture into the prepared tin and level the surface. Chill for several hours until set.

*7* To serve, turn the mousse out on to a plate and cut into slices or wedges. Serve the chocolate mousse on serving plates and spoon some of the glazed kumquats alongside.

--- VARIATION ---
Use peeled and sliced small, seedless oranges in place of the kumquats.

--- NUTRITION NOTES ---

Per portion:
| | |
|---|---|
| Energy | 432kcals/1810kJ |
| Fat, total | 22.3g |
|    saturated fat | 12g |
| Protein | 7.6g |
| Carbohydrate | 50.2g |
|    sugar, total | 49.8g |
| Fibre – NSP | 2.68g |
| Sodium | 68mg |

# Lemon Cheesecake with Forest Fruits

## INGREDIENTS

*Serves 8*

50g/2oz/4 tbsp unsalted butter
25g/1oz/2 tbsp light soft brown sugar
45ml/3 tbsp golden syrup
115g/4oz/generous 1 cup gluten-free
   cornflakes
11g/¼oz sachet powdered gelatine
225g/8oz/1 cup medium-fat
   soft cheese
150g/5oz/½ cup Greek yogurt
150ml/¼ pint/⅔ cup reduced-fat
   single cream
finely grated rind and juice of 2 lemons
75g/3oz/scant ½ cup caster sugar
2 eggs, separated
icing sugar, for dusting
225g/8oz mixed, prepared fresh forest
   fruits, such as blackberries, raspberries
   and redcurrants, to decorate

*1* Place the butter, brown sugar and syrup in a saucepan and heat over a low heat until the mixture has melted and is well blended, stirring. Remove from the heat and stir in the cornflakes.

*2* Press the mixture over the base of a deep 20cm/8in loose-bottomed, round cake tin. Chill for 30 minutes.

*3* Sprinkle the gelatine over 45ml/ 3 tbsp water in a bowl and leave to soak for a few minutes. Place the bowl over a pan of simmering water and stir until the gelatine has dissolved. Place the cheese, yogurt, cream, lemon rind and juice, caster sugar and egg yolks in a large bowl and beat until smooth and thoroughly mixed.

*4* Add the hot gelatine to the cheese and lemon mixture and beat until well mixed.

*5* Whisk the egg whites until stiff, then fold into the cheese mixture.

*6* Pour the cheese mixture over the cornflake base and gently level the surface. Chill for 4–5 hours until the filling has set. Carefully remove the cheesecake from the tin and place on a serving plate. Decorate with the mixed fresh fruits, dust with icing sugar and serve immediately in slices.

---

### VARIATION

Use unsweetened puffed rice cereal or rice crispies in place of the cornflakes.

---

### NUTRITION NOTES

Per portion:

| | |
|---|---|
| Energy | 297kcals/1246kJ |
| Fat, total | 15.2g |
| saturated fat | 6.65g |
| Protein | 8.9g |
| Carbohydrate | 33.2g |
| sugar, total | 22g |
| Fibre – NSP | 0.9g |
| Sodium | 267mg |

# Baked Fruit Compote

## INGREDIENTS

*Serves 6*

115g/4oz/⅔ cup ready-to-eat
    dried figs
115g/4oz/½ cup ready-to-eat
    dried apricots
50g/2oz/½ cup ready-to-eat dried
    apple rings
50g/2oz/¼ cup ready-to-eat prunes
50g/2oz/½ cup ready-to-eat
    dried pears
50g/2oz/½ cup ready-to-eat
    dried peaches
300ml/½ pint/1¼ cups unsweetened
    apple juice
300ml/½ pint/1¼ cups unsweetened
    orange juice
6 cloves
1 cinnamon stick
toasted flaked almonds, to decorate

*1* Preheat the oven to 180°C/350°F/
Gas 4. Place the figs, apricots, apple
rings, prunes, pears and peaches in a
shallow ovenproof dish and stir to mix.

*2* Mix together the apple and orange
juices and pour over the fruit. Add
the cloves and cinnamon stick and stir
gently to mix.

*3* Bake for about 30 minutes until the
fruit mixture is hot, stirring once
or twice during cooking. Set aside and
leave to soak for 20 minutes, then
remove and discard the cloves and
cinnamon stick.

*4* Spoon into serving bowls and serve
warm or cold, decorated with
toasted flaked almonds.

---
COOK'S TIP

Use other mixtures of unsweetened fruit
juices, such as pineapple and orange or
grape and apple.
---

---
NUTRITION NOTES

Per portion:
| | |
|---|---|
| Energy | 174kcals/744kJ |
| Fat, total | 0.8g |
|   saturated fat | 0.05g |
| Protein | 2.5g |
| Carbohydrate | 42.2g |
|   sugar, total | 42.1g |
| Fibre – NSP | 5.16g |
| Sodium | 26mg |
---

# Mango Yogurt Ice

## INGREDIENTS

*Serves 6*

450g/1lb ripe mango
    flesh, chopped
300ml/½ pint/1¼ cups low-fat peach
    or apricot yogurt
150ml/¼ pint/⅔ cup Greek yogurt
150ml/¼ pint/⅔ cup low-fat
    natural yogurt
25–50g/1–2oz/2–4 tbsp caster sugar
fresh mint sprigs, to decorate

*1* Place the mango flesh in a blender
or food processor and blend until
smooth. Transfer to a bowl.

*2* Add all three yogurts and blend
until thoroughly mixed.

*3* Stir in enough of the sugar to
sweeten to taste and stir to mix.

*4* Pour the mixture into a shallow,
plastic container. Cover and chill
for 1½–2 hours until it is mushy in
consistency. Turn the mixture into a
chilled bowl and beat until smooth.

*5* Return the mixture to the plastic
container, cover and freeze until
the ice is firm. Transfer the ice to the
fridge about 30 minutes before serving
to allow it to soften a little. Serve in
scoops decorated with mint sprigs.

---
NUTRITION NOTES

Per portion:
| | |
|---|---|
| Energy | 155kcals/655kJ |
| Fat, total | 2.9g |
|   saturated fat | 1.7g |
| Protein | 5.3g |
| Carbohydrate | 28.4g |
|   sugar, total | 24.3g |
| Fibre – NSP | 2.17g |
| Sodium | 89.6mg |
---

# Apricot and Almond Tart

Crumbly, rich gluten-free pastry encases an apricot and almond filling to make this tempting dessert. Serve with Greek yogurt or crème fraîche.

## Ingredients

*Serves 6*

115g/4oz/½ cup soft margarine
115g/4oz/½ cup caster sugar
1 egg, beaten
50g/2oz/⅓ cup ground rice
50g/2oz/½ cup ground almonds
few drops of almond essence
450g/1 lb fresh apricots, halved
    and stoned
sifted icing sugar, for dusting (optional)
apricot slices and fresh mint sprigs, to
    decorate (optional)

**For the pastry**

115g/4oz/1 cup brown rice flour
115g/4oz/1 cup gluten-free cornmeal
pinch of salt
115g/4oz/½ cup soft margarine
25g/1oz/2 tbsp caster sugar
1 egg yolk

*1* To make the pastry, place the rice flour, cornmeal and pinch of salt in a bowl and stir to mix. Lightly rub in the soft margarine until the mixture resembles breadcrumbs.

---

### Variation

For a change, use ground hazelnuts and vanilla essence in place of the ground almonds and almond essence.

---

*2* Add the sugar, stir in the egg yolk and add enough chilled water to make a smooth, soft but not sticky dough. Wrap the dough and chill for 30 minutes.

*3* Preheat the oven to 180°C/350°F/ Gas 4. Line a 24cm/9½in loose-bottomed flan tin with the pastry by pressing it gently over the base and up the sides of the tin, making sure there are no holes in the pastry. Trim the edge with a sharp knife.

*4* To make the almond filling, place the margarine and sugar in a mixing bowl and cream together, using a wooden spoon, ntil the mixture is light and fluffy.

*5* Gradually add the beaten egg, beating well after each addition. Fold in the ground rice and almonds and the almond essence and mix well to incorporate them.

*6* Spoon the almond mixture into the pastry case, spreading it evenly, then arrange the apricot halves cut side down on top.

*7* Place on a baking sheet and bake for 40–45 minutes until the filling and pastry are cooked and lightly browned. Serve warm or cold, dusted with icing sugar and decorated with apricots and sprigs of mint, if you like.

---

### Nutrition Notes

| Per portion: | |
|---|---|
| Energy | 487kcals/2029kJ |
| Fat, total | 29.6g |
| saturated fat | 5.67g |
| Protein | 5.6g |
| Carbohydrate | 50.4g |
| sugar, total | 22.8g |
| Fibre – NSP | 1.54g |
| Sodium | 212mg |

# BREADS, CAKES AND BAKES

*The aroma wafting from the oven when baking home-made breads and cakes is hard to resist. These wonderful recipes are all gluten-free — try Cheese and Onion Cornbread, a fabulous version of Victoria Sandwich Cake, Gingerbread and Country Apple Cake, or bake a batch of mouthwatering Apricot and Orange Muffins or Chocolate Chip Cookies, which make ideal treats and snacks for children and adults alike. Choose from this tempting selection and get baking!*

# Rice, Buckwheat and Corn Bread

Freshly baked, this wonderful bread is delicious served straight from the oven. Cut into thick slices and serve with fruit conserve or honey for breakfast.

## INGREDIENTS

### *Makes one 900g/2lb loaf*

200ml/7fl oz/scant 1 cup tepid semi-skimmed milk
200ml/7fl oz/scant 1 cup tepid water
350g/12oz/3 cups brown rice flour
50g/2oz/½ cup buckwheat flour or soya flour
50g/2oz/½ cup gluten-free cornmeal
5ml/1 tsp caster sugar
5ml/1 tsp salt
7g/¼oz sachet easy-blend dried yeast
40g/1½oz/3 tbsp soft margarine
1 medium egg, beaten, plus extra for glazing
30ml/2 tbsp sesame seeds

---
COOK'S TIP
---

You can bake the bread in a different-shaped tin, such as a deep round or square cake tin, if preferred.

---
NUTRITION NOTES
---

Per loaf:

| | |
|---|---|
| Energy | 2200kcals/9188kJ |
| Fat, total | 59g |
| saturated fat | 12g |
| Protein | 62g |
| Carbohydrate | 344g |
| sugar, total | 21g |
| Fibre – NSP | 14g |
| Sodium | 493mg |

*1* Lightly grease a 900g/2lb loaf tin. Mix the milk and water together in a measuring jug.

*2* Place the rice flour, buckwheat or soya flour, cornmeal, sugar and salt in a bowl and stir in the dried yeast. Mix well until all the ingredients are combined, then lightly rub in the margarine until the mixture resembles fine breadcrumbs.

*3* Add the milk and water mixture and the egg and beat together to form a smooth, thick consistency.

*4* Spoon the mixture into the prepared tin, then cover and leave in a warm place until it has risen to the top of the tin.

*5* Preheat the oven to 200°C/400°F/ Gas 6. Brush the top of the bread with a little beaten egg and scatter the sesame seeds over it. Bake for about 30 minutes until lightly browned. Run a knife all round the edge of the tin to loosen the loaf.

*6* Turn out the bread on to a wire rack to cool slightly and serve warm. Alternatively, leave on the rack until completely cold, then cut into slices. To store, wrap the loaf in foil or seal in a plastic bag.

# Cheese and Onion Cornbread

Full of flavour, this gluten-free cornbread is delicious served freshly baked, warm or cold in slices, either on its own or spread with a little low-fat spread. It makes an ideal accompaniment to soups, stews and chillies.

## INGREDIENTS

*Makes one 900g/2lb loaf*

15ml/1 tbsp sunflower oil
1 onion, thinly sliced
175g/6oz/1½ cups gluten-free
  cornmeal
75g/3oz/¾ cup rice flour
25g/1oz/¼ cup soya flour
15ml/1 tbsp gluten-free baking powder
5ml/1 tsp caster sugar
5ml/1 tsp salt
115g/4oz/1 cup coarsely grated mature
  Cheddar cheese
200ml/7fl oz/scant 1 cup tepid milk
2 eggs
40g/1½oz/3 tbsp soft
  margarine, melted

---
#### COOK'S TIP

Reserve a little of the grated cheese and cooked onion and scatter it over the top of the bread before baking.

---

*1* Preheat the oven to 190°C/375°F/ Gas 5. Lightly grease a 900g/2lb loaf tin. Heat the oil in a frying pan, add the onion and cook gently for 10–15 minutes until softened, stirring occasionally. Remove from the heat and set aside to cool.

*2* Place the cornmeal, rice flour, soya flour, baking powder, sugar and salt in a bowl and combine thoroughly. Stir in the cheese, mixing well.

*3* Beat together the milk, eggs and melted margarine. Add to the flour mixture and mix well.

*4* Stir in the cooled, cooked onions and mix again.

*5* Spoon the onion mixture into the prepared tin, level the surface and bake for about 30 minutes until the bread has risen and is golden brown.

*6* Run a knife around the edge to loosen the loaf. Turn out on to a wire rack to cool slightly and serve warm. Alternatively, leave it on the rack until completely cold, then cut into slices. To store the loaf, wrap it in foil or seal in a plastic bag.

---
#### NUTRITION NOTES

Per loaf:

| | |
|---|---|
| Energy | 2314kcals/9631kJ |
| Fat, total | 121g |
| saturated fat | 42g |
| Protein | 83g |
| Carbohydrate | 220g |
| sugar, total | 21.2g |
| Fibre – NSP | 9g |
| Sodium | 3100mg |

# Sultana and Cinnamon Chewy Bars

These spicy, chewy bars are hard to resist and make a great treat, especially for children.

### INGREDIENTS

*Makes 16*
115g/4oz/½ cup soft margarine
25g/1oz/2 tbsp light soft brown sugar
25g/1oz plain toffees
50g/2oz/¼ cup clear honey
175g/6oz/1½ cups sultanas
10ml/2 tsp ground cinnamon
175g/6oz gluten-free rice crispies

*1* Lightly grease a shallow 23 x 28cm/9 x 11in cake tin. Place the margarine, sugar, toffees and honey in a saucepan and heat gently until melted, stirring. Bring to the boil, then remove the pan from the heat.

*2* Stir in the sultanas, cinnamon and rice crispies and mix well. Transfer the mixture to the prepared tin and spread the mixture evenly, pressing it down firmly.

*3* Leave to cool, then chill until firm. Once firm, cut into bars, remove from the tin and serve. Store the bars in an airtight container in the fridge.

---

— VARIATION —

For an extra-special treat, melt 75g/3oz plain or milk chocolate and spread or, using a teaspoon or paper piping bag, drizzle it over the cold rice crispie mixture. Leave to set before cutting into bars.

---

— NUTRITION NOTES —

Per bar:

| | |
|---|---|
| Energy | 145kcals/610kJ |
| Fat, total | 6.4g |
| saturated fat | 1.4g |
| Protein | 1g |
| Carbohydrate | 22.4g |
| sugar, total | 13.4g |
| Fibre – NSP | 0.3g |
| Sodium | 1.95mg |

---

# Apricot and Orange Muffins

Serve these fruity muffins freshly baked and warm.

### INGREDIENTS

*Makes 8 large or 12 medium muffins*
115g/4oz/1 cup gluten-free cornmeal
75g/3oz/¾ cup rice flour
15ml/1 tbsp gluten-free baking powder
pinch of salt
50g/2oz/4 tbsp soft margarine, melted
50g/2oz/¼ cup light soft brown sugar
1 egg, beaten
200ml/7fl oz/scant 1 cup semi-skimmed milk
finely grated rind of 1 orange
115g/4oz/½ cup ready-to-eat dried apricots, chopped

*1* Preheat the oven to 200°C/400°F/ Gas 6. Lightly grease or line eight or 12 muffin tins or deep bun tins. Place the cornmeal, rice flour, baking powder and salt in a bowl and mix.

*2* Stir together the melted margarine, sugar, egg, milk and orange rind, then pour the mixture over the dry ingredients. Fold the ingredients gently together – just enough to combine them. The mixture will look quite lumpy, which is correct, as over-mixing will result in heavy muffins.

*3* Fold in the chopped dried apricots, then spoon the mixture into the prepared muffin or bun tins, dividing it equally among them.

*4* Bake for 15–20 minutes until the muffins have risen and are golden brown and springy to the touch. Turn them out on to a wire rack to cool.

*5* Serve the muffins warm or cold, on their own or cut in half and spread with a little low-fat spread. Store in an airtight container for up to one week or seal in plastic bags and freeze for up to three months.

---

— NUTRITION NOTES —

Per medium muffin:

| | |
|---|---|
| Energy | 136kcals/572kJ |
| Fat, total | 4.6g |
| saturated fat | 1g |
| Protein | 2.9g |
| Carbohydrate | 21g |
| sugar, total | 8.5g |
| Fibre – NSP | 0.9g |
| Sodium | 195mg |

# Victoria Sandwich Cake

Serve this light, gluten-free equivalent of the classic sponge cake sandwiched together with your favourite jam. For special occasions, fill the cake with prepared fresh fruit, such as raspberries or sliced peaches, as well as jam and whipped dairy cream or fromage frais.

## INGREDIENTS

*Makes one 18cm/7in cake*

175g/6oz/¾ cup soft margarine
175g/6oz/¾ cup caster sugar
3 eggs, beaten
175g/6oz/1½ cups gluten-free self-raising flour, sifted
60ml/4 tbsp jam
150ml/¼ pint/⅔ cup whipped cream or fromage frais
15–30ml/1–2 tbsp icing sugar, for dusting

| NUTRITION NOTES | |
|---|---|
| **Per cake:** | |
| Energy | 3140kcals/13110kJ |
| Fat, total | 166g |
| saturated fat | 36g |
| Protein | 35g |
| Carbohydrate | 391g |
| sugar, total | 263g |
| Fibre – NSP | 0g |
| Sodium | 1486mg |

*1* Preheat the oven to 180°C/350°F/ Gas 4. Lightly grease and base-line two 18cm/7in sandwich tins.

*2* Place the margarine and caster sugar in a bowl and cream together until pale and fluffy.

*3* Add the eggs, a little at a time, beating well after each addition. Fold in half the flour, using a metal spoon, then fold in the rest.

---
VARIATION

Replace 30ml/2 tbsp of the flour with sifted gluten-free cocoa powder. Sandwich the cakes with chocolate butter icing.

*4* Divide the mixture evenly between the two sandwich tins and level the surface with the back of a spoon.

*5* Bake for 25–30 minutes until the cakes have risen, feel just firm to the touch and are golden brown. Turn out and cool on a wire rack.

*6* When the cakes are cool, sandwich them with the jam and whipped cream or fromage frais. Dust the top of the cake with sifted icing sugar and serve cut into slices. Store the cake in the fridge in an airtight container or wrapped in foil.

# Fruit, Nut and Seed Teabread

Cut into slices and spread with a little low fat spread, jam or honey, this teabread makes an ideal breakfast bread.

## INGREDIENTS

*Makes one 900g/2lb loaf*

115g/4oz/⅔ cup dried dates, chopped
115g/4oz/½ cup ready-to-eat dried apricots, chopped
115g/4oz/1 cup sultanas
115g/4oz/½ cup light soft brown sugar
225g/8oz/2 cups gluten-free self-raising flour
5ml/1 tsp gluten-free baking powder
10ml/2 tsp mixed spice
75g/3oz/¾ cup chopped mixed nuts, such as walnuts and hazelnuts
75g/3oz/¾ cup mixed seeds, such as millet, sunflower and sesame seeds
2 eggs, beaten
150ml/¼ pint/⅔ cup semi-skimmed milk

---— NUTRITION NOTES —---

Per loaf:

| | |
|---|---|
| Energy | 3022kcals/12686kJ |
| Fat, total | 107g |
| saturated fat | 14g |
| Protein | 70.4g |
| Carbohydrate | 470g |
| sugar, total | 294g |
| Fibre – NSP | 20g |
| Sodium | 944mg |

*1* Preheat the oven to 180°C/350°F/ Gas 4. Lightly grease a 900g/2lb loaf tin. Place the chopped dates and apricots and sultanas in a large mixing bowl and stir in the sugar.

*2* Place the flour, baking powder, spice, mixed nuts and seeds in a separate bowl and mix well.

*3* Stir the eggs and milk into the fruit, then add the flour mixture and beat together until well mixed.

*4* Spoon into the prepared tin and level the surface. Bake for about 1 hour until the teabread is firm to the touch and lightly browned.

*5* Allow to cool in the tin for a few minutes, then turn out on to a wire rack to cool completely. Serve warm or cold, cut into slices, either on its own or spread with low-fat spread and jam. Wrap the teabread in foil to store.

# Gingerbread

## INGREDIENTS

*Makes one 900g/2lb loaf*

115g/4oz/½ cup light soft brown sugar
75g/3oz/6 tbsp soft margarine
75g/3oz/¼ cup golden syrup
75g/3oz/¼ cup black treacle
105ml/7 tbsp semi-skimmed milk
1 egg, beaten
175g/6oz/1½ cups gluten-free
    plain flour
50g/2oz/½ cup gram flour
pinch of salt
10ml/2 tsp ground ginger
5ml/1 tsp ground cinnamon
7.5ml/1½ tsp gluten-free
    baking powder

*1* Preheat the oven to 160°C/325°F/ Gas 3. Lightly grease and line a 900g/2lb loaf tin. Place the sugar, margarine, syrup and treacle in a saucepan and heat gently until melted and blended, stirring occasionally.

*2* Remove the pan from the heat, leave to cool slightly, then mix in the milk and egg.

*3* Mix the flours, salt, spices and baking powder in a large bowl.

*4* Make a well in the centre, pour in the liquid mixture and beat well.

*5* Pour the mixture into the prepared tin and bake for 1–1¼ hours until firm to the touch and lightly browned.

*6* Allow to cool in the tin for a few minutes, then turn out on to a wire rack to cool completely. Store it in an airtight container or wrapped in foil.

---

NUTRITION NOTES

Per loaf:

| | |
|---|---|
| Energy | 2168kcals/9100kJ |
| Fat, total | 73g |
| saturated fat | 16g |
| Protein | 25g |
| Carbohydrate | 375g |
| sugar, total | 240g |
| Fibre – NSP | 0g |
| Sodium | 1915mg |

---

VARIATION

Fold 50g/2oz finely chopped preserved stem ginger into the raw cake mixture, if liked. Add 5–10ml/1–2 tsp extra ground ginger for a more pronounced flavour.

# Chocolate Chip Cookies

## Ingredients

*Makes 16*

75g/3oz/6 tbsp soft margarine
50g/2oz/¼ cup light soft brown sugar
50g/2oz/¼ cup caster sugar
1 egg, beaten
few drops of vanilla essence
75g/3oz/¾ cup rice flour
75g/3oz/¾ cup gluten-free cornmeal
5ml/1 tsp gluten-free baking powder
pinch of salt
115g/4oz/⅔ cup plain chocolate chips,
   or a mixture of milk and white
   chocolate chips

*1* Preheat the oven to 190°C/375°F/
Gas 5. Lightly grease two baking
sheets. Place the margarine and sugars
in a bowl and cream together until light
and fluffy.

*2* Beat in the egg and vanilla essence.
Fold in the rice flour, cornmeal,
baking powder and salt, then fold in
the chocolate chips.

*3* Place spoonfuls of the mixture on
the prepared baking sheets, leaving
space for spreading between each one.
Bake for 10–15 minutes until the
cookies are lightly browned.

*4* Remove the cookies from the
oven and leave to cool for a few
minutes, then transfer to a wire rack
using a palette knife and leave to cool
completely before serving. Once cold,
store the cookies in an airtight
container for up to a week, or pack
into plastic bags and freeze.

| NUTRITION NOTES | |
| --- | --- |
| Per portion: | |
| Energy | 135kcals/567kJ |
| Fat, total | 6.5g |
|   saturated fat | 2.12g |
| Protein | 1.6g |
| Carbohydrate | 18.3g |
|   sugar, total | 10.9g |
| Fibre – NSP | 0.37g |
| Sodium | 75mg |

# Cherry Coconut Munchies

You'll find it hard to stop at just
one of these munchies, which
make a wonderful morning or
afternoon treat. If liked, drizzle
25–50g/1–2oz melted chocolate
over the cold munchies and leave
to set before serving.

## Ingredients

*Makes 20*

2 egg whites
115g/4oz/1 cup icing sugar, sifted
115g/4oz/1 cup ground almonds
115g/4oz/generous 1 cup desiccated
   coconut
few drops of almond essence
75g/3oz/⅓ cup glacé cherries,
   finely chopped

*1* Preheat the oven to 150°C/300°F/
Gas 2. Line two baking sheets with
non-stick baking paper. Place the egg
whites in a bowl and whisk until stiff.

*2* Fold in the icing sugar, then fold in
the ground almonds, coconut and
almond essence to form a sticky dough.
Fold in the chopped cherries.

| NUTRITION NOTES | |
| --- | --- |
| Per portion: | |
| Energy | 103kcals/430kJ |
| Fat, total | 6.7g |
|   saturated fat | 3.3g |
| Protein | 1.83g |
| Carbohydrate | 9.3g |
|   sugar, total | 9.1g |
| Fibre – NSP | 1.24g |
| Sodium | 10.2mg |

*3* Place heaped teaspoonfuls of the
mixture on the prepared baking
sheets. Bake for 25 minutes until pale
golden. Cool on the baking sheets for a
few minutes, then transfer to a wire
rack until cold. Store in an airtight
container for up to a week.

| VARIATIONS |
| --- |
| Use ground hazelnuts in place of the almonds and omit the almond essence. |

# Country Apple Cake

## INGREDIENTS

*Makes one 18cm/7in cake*

115g/4oz/½ cup soft margarine
115g/4oz/½ cup light soft brown sugar
2 eggs, beaten
115g/4oz/1 cup gluten-free self-raising
   flour, sifted
50g/2oz/½ cup rice flour
5ml/1 tsp gluten-free baking powder
10ml/2 tsp mixed spice
1 medium cooking apple, peeled, cored
   and chopped
115g/4oz/1 cup raisins
about 60ml/4 tbsp semi-skimmed milk
15g/½oz/2 tbsp flaked almonds
custard or ice cream, to serve
   (optional)

*1* Preheat the oven to 160°C/325°F/
Gas 3. Lightly grease and line a
deep 18cm/7in round, loose-bottomed
cake tin.

*2* Place the margarine and sugar in a
bowl and cream together until pale
and fluffy. Gradually add the eggs,
beating well after each addition. Fold in
the flour, rice flour, baking powder and
mixed spice and mix well.

—— VARIATIONS ——

Use sultanas or chopped ready-to-eat dried
apricots or pears instead of the raisins.

*3* Fold in the chopped apple, raisins
and enough milk to make a soft,
dropping consistency.

*4* Turn the mixture into the prepared
tin and level the surface. Sprinkle
the flaked almonds over the top. Bake
for 1–1¼ hours until risen, firm to the
touch and golden brown.

*5* Cool in the tin for about
10 minutes, then turn out on to a
wire rack to cool. Cut into slices when
cold. Alternatively, serve warm, in
slices, with custard or ice cream. Store
the cold cake in an airtight container or
wrapped in foil.

—— NUTRITION NOTES ——

Per cake:

| | |
|---|---|
| Energy | 2506kcals/10483kJ |
| Fat, total | 120g |
| saturated fat | 25g |
| Protein | 35g |
| Carbohydrate | 340g |
| sugar, total | 214g |
| Fibre – NSP | 6g |
| Sodium | 1695mg |

# INFORMATION FILE

## USEFUL ADDRESSES

**Action against Allergy**
PO Box 278
Twickenham
Middlesex TW1 4QQ

**Canadian Coeliac Association**
6519B Mississauga Road
Mississauga
Ontario L5N 1A6
Tel: (1) 905 567 7195

**The Coeliac Society of Australia**
PO Box 271
Wahroonga 2076 NSW
Tel: (61) 29411 4100

**The Coeliac Society of Great Britain**
PO Box 220
High Wycombe
Bucks HP11 2HY
Tel: 01494 437278

**The Coeliac Society of South Africa**
Box No 64203
Highland North 2073
Johannesburg
Tel: (27) 11 440 3431

## SUPERMARKET SERVICES

Many supermarket chains offer a free advice service for people with food allergies or intolerances. Most publish lists of their own-brand foods that are gluten-free. Wheat-free food lists are also available.

## MAIL-ORDER COMPANIES SUPPLYING GLUTEN-FREE FOODS

Larkhall Green Farm
225 Putney Bridge Road
London SW15 2PY
Tel: 0181 874 1130

Lifestyle Healthcare Limited
Centenary Business Park
Henley-on-Thames
Oxfordshire RG9 1DS
Tel: 01491 411767

Doves Farm Foods Ltd
Salisbury Road
Hungerford
Berkshire RG17 0RF
Tel: 01488 684880

Gluten-Free Foods Ltd
Unit 10
Honeypot Business Park
Parr Road
Stanmore
Middlesex HA7 1NL
Tel: 0181 952 0052

Nutricia Dietary Products Ltd
Newmarket Avenue
White Horse Business Park
Trowbridge
Wiltshire BA14 0XQ
Tel: 01225 711801

## FURTHER READING

Austin, Jean, Simmonds, Jill and Lambourne, Angela (eds), *The Coeliac Cookbook* (The Coeliac Society, 1997)
Coultate, T. P., *Food – The Chemistry of its Components* (The Royal Society of Chemistry, 1996)
Geer, Rita, *Recipes for Health – Gluten-free,* (Thorsons, 1995)
*Living without Gluten* (booklet, Nutricia Diet Products, 1997)
Nilson, Bee, *The Coeliac Handbook* (the Coeliac Society, 1997)
Noble, Joan, *The Nutricia Wheat and Gluten-Free Cookbook* (Vermillion, 1996)
Thomas, Briony (ed), *Manual of Dietetic Practice* (Blackwell Science, 1994)
Thompson, Peter, *Gluten-Free Cookery* (Hodder and Stoughton, 1995)

*The Inside Story on Food and Health*
Subscription magazine with general information on diet and nutrition.
Available from:
Berrydales Publishers
Berrydale House
5 Lawn Road
London NW3 2XS
Tel: 0171 722 2866

## GLOSSARY OF BASIC TERMS

**Anaemia** – a shortage or deficiency of red blood cells that leads to lack of energy and shortness of breath.
**Coeliac** – a person suffering from the condition known as coeliac disease.
**Coeliac disease** – a condition caused by a sensitivity to gluten.
**Dermatitis herpetiformis** – a rare skin condition caused by a sensitivity to gluten. It causes an extremely itchy skin rash.
**Gluten** – a type of protein that is present in wheat and rye.
**Gluten-free diet** – a strict diet, which excludes all foods that contain gluten, such as wheat and rye, and foods such as barley and oats, which contain similar proteins to gluten.
**Jejunal biopsy** – a test performed under light sedation, which involves removing a small piece of villi from the lining of the small intestine. Microscopic examination reveals whether the coeliac condition is present.
**Nutrients** – essential dietary substances that include energy (kilocalories/kilojoules), protein, fat, fibre, carbohydrate, vitamins and minerals.
**Villi** – thread-like projections that cover the lining of the small intestine and are responsible for the absorption of food.
**Wheat allergy and intolerance** – a condition that can cause a wide range of symptoms and is treated by following a strict gluten-free diet that excludes all sources of wheat, wheat protein and wheat starch.

# INDEX

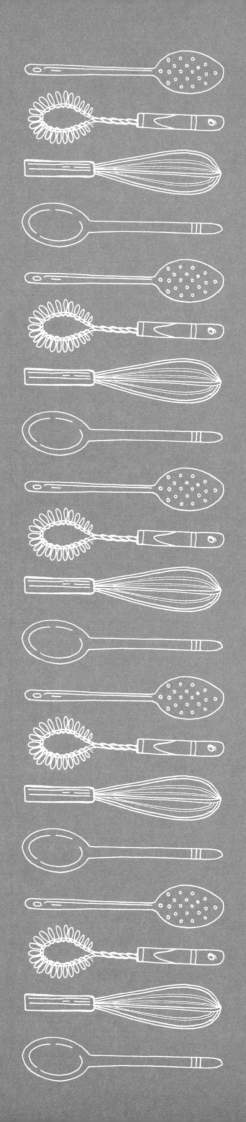